Keys of Knowledge

H.E. Tarthang Rinpoche

Keys of Knowledge

Tarthang Tulku

Dharma Publishing

UNDERSTANDING SELF AND MIND

Knowledge of Freedom: Time to Change
Revelations of Mind
Dimensions of Mind
Keys of Knowledge

ISBN: 978-0-89800-091-7
Library of Congress Control Number: 2016951428

Printed in the USA by Dharma Mangalam Press, Ratna Ling, 35755 Hauser Bridge Road, Cazadero, CA 95421

10 9 8 7 6 5 4 3 2 1

Dedicated to my students,
and to the living possibility
of a Western Dharma tradition

Contents

Topics by Chapter

Here is a list of key topics addressed in each chapter, with page numbers for ease of study.

Prologue: Mind Holds the Keys

Chapter One: Going

Chapter Two: Knowing

Chapter Three: Ruling

Chapter Four: Kingdom of Time

Chapter Five: Play of Light

Chapter Six: Mind at Ease

Chapter Seven: We Embody Knowledge

Chapter Eight: The Great Journey

Prologue:
Mind Holds
the Keys

These essays began life as addresses given during a special two-week conference I held for my longtime students to celebrate the 240th anniversary of the birth of America, my gracious adopted country.

The conference was held at the Ratna Ling Retreat Center in Northern California. Ratna Ling means 'Jewel Crest'; like a jewel in the talons of a dragon, it lies just south of the winding coastal ridge that holds the Odiyan Copper Mountain Retreat Center, the site of many important Dharma projects.

Every July, I meet with students from all over the world for seminars and practice. During these events I try to open up ideas and approaches to help us refine our understanding of who we are, what we are doing, and what part we have to play in the unfolding of human knowledge.

The essence of what I try to impart to my students during these events is that the human mission, our true purpose here, is wholeness. Wholeness is never wholly for ourselves. For real wholeness is always communicated to others, in spreading ripples of positive influence and deep appreciation.

I do not believe this mission is only for my own students. It awaits all of us sentient beings, as we begin to understand ourselves and transform our experience.

I have lived in the United States for nearly forty-eight years now. I have had relatively little formal training in the specialized modes of knowledge that are part of Western culture, but I have had lots of experience with Western people—with their dreams and ideals, with their concepts and models, with their knowledge. Over the years I have interacted with thousands of Westerners, from scientists, engineers and financial managers, to teachers, builders, and artists.

In the process, I have made a careful study of the Western mind, exploring the special strengths and unique orientations that are its hallmarks. I discovered that it was rare for Westerners to feel comfortable within their own skins. I encountered chronic forms of mental suffering that took shape as skepticism, disappointment, and frustration, and specific cognitive and cultural patterns that often led to interpersonal tension and deep dissatisfaction with the self, 'the one who' seems to architect all the pain within.

As I learned from the people around me, I in turn found myself called upon to share what I knew.

I am in a unique position as the director, manager, and Head Lama of the Tibetan Nyingma Meditation Center. As I try to carry out my role, I constantly think of my own teachers, who offered me, with unfailing kindness, a beautiful model of conduct and a vision of the real potentials of the mind.

Here, hard at work on the Dharma projects that have absorbed my attention for close on fifty years, I am only myself, an ordinary human being who was once a penniless refugee. Still, I feel it's my duty to uphold their example if I can, and so I try my best to help.

There are as many different opinions and positions as there are minds, and it can be hard to find harmony. Westerners in particular display attitudes that can be traced back to their native cultures, cultures that resolutely promote the importance of each individual going his own way.

With so many conditions, so much individual chemistry in play, we don't always get along well. We have different approaches to tasks, different priorities, different areas of strength and weakness. When these fail to mesh, conflicts emerge.

If we address our conflicts without a clear understanding and appreciation of the differences from which they derive, biases can form, even against those who are quite close to us in attitude and belief. These biases can profoundly attenuate our ability to act effectively in the world, and to recognize the beauty and potential of our fellow human beings.

There are deeper consequences, too, for our prejudices stem from a much more fundamental bias that shapes our every thought and perception, dictating 'good for me' and 'bad for me.' Everything we know appears to us mediated by such judgments, and as a result we can become alienated from our own experience.

Throughout our lives, our desires press in on us, demanding, yearning, hungry; our fears and aversions drive us along. Trapped between judgments, we long for peace and fulfillment, but again and again our experiences bring us pain. Through no fault of our own, from the moment we are born, we find ourselves forced to march down this road. To be human, according to this prescribed pathway, is to live in a world that endures severe shortages of happiness.

To solve these problems, we will need to provide a new atmosphere; we will need to change the internal conditions under which the mind operates.

In order to do that, we need to understand them.

Since my earliest years, my life has been shaped by the Dharma. I remember as a young child studying texts and language with my father and with a special tutor. When I was about nine, I went to Tarthang Monastery, and for five years I received training there. Starting at the age of fourteen, I traveled to study with other teachers, first in the Golok region of Eastern Tibet and then with the great masters of Khams.

It was there that I met my root master, the knowledge-holder Jamyang Khyentse Chokyi Lodro; the great Nyingma lineage holders Zhechen Kongtrul and Zhechen Rabjam the Sixth; and many other celebrated teachers.

In my early twenties, I went to study at Adzom Gar, where my principal teacher was A-'gyur Rinpoche, one of the most important Dzogchen masters of the twentieth century. This great teacher embodied a very pure lineage of transmitted understanding that reached back to the beginning of the Tibetan Buddhist world; there is no one like him alive today.

Adzom Gar had been founded by A-'gyur Rinpoche's father Adzom Drugpa, a disciple of the nineteenth century masters Jamyang Khyentse Wangpo and Patrul Rinpoche. A-'gyur was Adzom Drugpa's lineage heir as well as his son. This remarkably gentle man held deep insight into the operations of mind, and an undeniable power of realization that was far beyond that of ordinary people.

It was through the tireless efforts of masters like A-'gyur Rinpoche that my fellow students and I began to recognize the full extent of the power of mind, the real nature of the shackles we wear as sentient beings, and what it might mean to throw off those shackles.

From the perspective of the Buddhas, the world with its *dhatus* or elements comes from the Dharmadhatu, the primordial field of space that manifests as specific shapes and forms. Mind and mental events emerge in the same way. The Abhidharma speaks of fifty-one or more mental events, while the Vijnanavadins identified eighty topics or shapes of the mind. Usually we reduce these to eight basic modes of consciousness, but if we look in more detail, we can identify such elements as the six root emotions: greed, hatred, ignorance, clinging to views, pride, and doubt.

At a more fundamental level, it can be helpful to see the emotions, or *kleshas*, as manifestations of 'I-ness' and 'self-ness'. From this foundation emerge the structures of causality, time, and the six sense faculties. A dynamic is activated in which the mind flickers back and forth in endless juxtaposed oppositions: good and bad, pro and con.

The teachings of the Vijnanavada and Yogachara schools have a great deal to teach us about these patternings of the mind. Western scholars who study the Mahayana have mostly given greater attention to the Madhyamaka school and its founder Nagarjuna, but there is a growing realization that the teachings preserved by the Yogachara are of fundamental importance. It is sometimes said—especially among Japanese scholars—that while Nagarjuna focused on the realm of the absolute, the Yogachara masters also investigated the realm of relative truth, and it is there that we live out our lives.

My Nyingma tradition has always given special emphasis to the Yogachara teachings. In the eighth century, when Buddhism was being established in Tibet, the famous scholar Shantarakshita brought to Tibet his own synthesis of Yogachara and Madhyamaka, which was strongly influenced by Yogachara's founder, Asanga.

The Yogachara asks penetrating questions: who experiences, how experience arises and how it is received, and how the relative relates to the absolute. Of these explorations, Shantarakshita was master.

Shantarakshita's teachings investigate the building blocks of the mind captivated by *samsara*, the endless round of cause and effect in which sentient beings live out their lives. They examine the realm of the mind and the nature of the objective world. They show how the truths of the Dharma interact with the manifestations of the ordinary mind, and how they may be perceived by the understanding of sentient beings trapped in samsaric consciousness.

Because Shantarakshita was able to make a bridge from the realm of sublime truth back to ordinary reality, his teachings can bring ordinary human beings into contact with *don-dam bden-pa*, absolute truth, revealing the perfect unity or co-existence of the relative and the absolute, of emptiness and form.

Deeply learned, accomplished in both logic and yogic realization, Shantarakshita passed on these teachings to the thirty-eighth king of Tibet, Dharmaraja Trisong Detsen. To Tibet's great good fortune, Shantarakshita's clear understanding laid out the path, creating a framework of study and practice for Tibetan Buddhists that held firm for more than a thousand years.

Still, these advanced teachings could not counter the many obstacles that arose to the founding of the Dharma in the Land of Snow. This task, Shantarakshita understood, would need more than the mastery of the Sutras and the determination of a powerful king. It would require the power of the Mantrayana path, the understanding of which transmuted negativity with no remainder, and cut off suffering at the root.

Realizing this, Shantarakshita asked the king to invite the Great Guru Padmasambhava—the Lo-

11

tus-Born One, who appeared in the world eight years after the Buddha's Parinirvana, his coming predicted by the Buddha himself.

With perfect knowledge of the Mantrayana's Diamond Vehicle, Padmasambhava possessed the power needed to subdue ancient, entrenched forces in the land that were hostile to the Dharma. In the chronicles it is said that the Great Guru was able to work directly with these energies, binding Tibet's tutelary deities with unbreakable vows of service. The transformation of Tibet's spiritual atmosphere also affected the followers of Tibet's indigenous shamanistic religion, who were deeply reluctant to give up their secular and spiritual power.

As these elements in Tibetan culture shifted, the Dharma could at last take hold.

The Lotus-Born Master brought a great treasure to Tibet, for he had the ability to train his most accomplished students in the path that leads to enlightenment in a single lifetime, and before he departed Tibet, he passed on his heart teachings to his twenty-five chief disciples.

According to the old chronicles, these unsurpassed practitioners possessed great powers, such as the ability to fly or to pass through solid rock, or—in the case of Lady Yeshe Tsogyal—to restore the dead to life. The twenty-five disciples would later take rebirth as the Thousand Tertons, or treasure-revealers, starting with Nyangral Nyima Odzer in the twelfth century and continuing through to legendary masters of Eastern Tibet such as Jamyang Khyentse Wangpo, Jamgon Kongtrul Lodro Thaye, and Chogyur Dechen Lingpa.

These three teachers took it upon themselves to protect the *terma*, the treasure-teachings of Padmasambhava recovered over the centuries by the Tertons. Working with the sublime insights provided by Jamyang Khyentse Wangpo and Chogyur Lingpa, Jamgon Kongtrul compiled the Rinchen Terdzod, a masterwork that brought together thousands of preserved texts.

It was these teachings that I received, in the early 1950s, from the Venerable Zhechen Rabjams the Sixth, who stood in the direct line of the heirs of these incomparable masters.

These treasure-teachings, little-known in the West, have tremendous spiritual power, for they carry the current of Padmasambhava's matchless insight; in all their myriad forms they express the power of that wave. They are therefore very precious, for students who practice the terma with devotion can be liberated in a single lifetime.

Although we are not Tertons, as we proceed on the path, we, too, can discover this same internal treasure, this same magical chariot, the Dharma of the Dharmadhatu. For all the forms our practice takes can be understood as manifestations of Bodhichitta, or enlightened mind.

In Buddhist thought, enlightenment manifests as a unity of compassion and wisdom. When compassion and wisdom are inseparably united, sentient beings are freed from bias; they enter bliss. Those who cultivate this unity are called Bodhisattvas.

The greatest Bodhisattvas function in the ordinary world as examples, leaders, uniquely gifted and powerful in their understanding. We who are Buddhists follow the path they show us, as best we can; we struggle, strive, and aspire. But Bodhisattvas *themselves* hold open a luminous potential, for they know beyond a doubt that all sentient beings, without exception, are capable of embodying, *just as they do*, the full expression of Bodhichitta.

The understanding that Bodhichitta's beautiful potential is expressed simultaneously in aspiration and fulfillment—that the journey and the destination are one and the same—lay at the heart of my masters' teachings.

Here are my roots; here is the source of my understanding. Yet the terms and concepts I present in this book are not themselves precisely Buddhist. In these pieces I have tried to adapt what I was taught in ways that might open up its relevance to Western readers. I have tried to use what I have learned of the Western mind to create a more accessible pathway that does not require prior training in Buddhism, or even any special kind of belief. Instead, it is my hope that the ideas in this book will apply more or less directly to experience the way that it is lived in the West.

These essays, then, are a record of my thoughts and reflections, the fruit of my years of study with my teachers and my time in America. They are all quite short, as they were originally intended as presentations to spark further dialogues among my students. As a result, there are many points upon which I touched only lightly, as there was no scope for greater elaboration.

When viewed from the open field of knowledge, so-called 'ordinary' mind presents an extraordinary opportunity to gather treasures far richer than what we are conditioned to believe ourselves capable of grasping.

For readers who would like to pursue these subjects more deeply, I want to assure you that it is possible to take these studies much further than we have gone here. Try to apply the method to the operations of your own mind; let your intrinsic intelligence open up its own limitations, its own structures. I promise that you are more than capable of the inquiry.

The enlightened ones who left their traces in history are more than names. They are more than ideas, or ideals: they inhabited the world. They had bodies and minds, and spoke as we do.

What *they* were, *we* can be too.

These essays are based upon a set of talks I dictated on interrelated topics of mind, language and time between February and June of 2016. Julia Witwer and Jack Petranker compiled the talks and edited the English. Each essay is prefaced by a short introduction that suggests points of entry, attitudes to keep in mind, and ways to apply the sometimes difficult concepts presented in each chapter of this book.

While the editors have done their best, further work is needed in English to develop language that could someday be adequate to the task of expressing the special forms of knowledge embodied by my masters. The material presented in this book will need to be elaborated and explored as I continue to seek ways to communicate what I have learned.

Readers might notice the appearance throughout the essays of dialogues, in which 'I', 'Me', 'Mine' and 'Mind' all have speaking parts. While these characters can at times say humorous things, the part they play in our lives is very serious, for they serve as the primary gatekeepers of the human condition. I hope that you will be able to create new dialogues in the light of what you discover here, new conversations of mind with mind that can lead us beyond the confining roles prescribed for us thus far.

Even though we have lived our lives within these confines, we have reason to rejoice. We have bodies, minds, and the language to communicate growing understanding. We have tools that will allow us to explore our experience. We can bring fresh air and light to the mind. And we can share what we discover with others.

As ordinary people, we tend to focus on ourselves; "My pain is my own," we say. And yet every one of us experiences 'my own', and all the pain that *my owning* entails. Even if our individual problems are solved, what about those of our friends and loved ones? We are the same; we share the same pain. What makes a difference for us might make a difference for them, too.

True understanding awakens compassion, awakens it without fail. From this sublime knowledge of the heart, love for all beings arises spontaneously, inevitably, sure as sunrise. May it inspire new visions of human potential in all who read this book.

Chapter One: Going

Introduction to Chapter One

Every civilization develops its own distinctive way of understanding, its own forms of knowledge. Just as different religions build different styles of temples or churches, so each culture forms its own religion and philosophy, its own science and ethics, its own customs.

As these forms of knowledge unfold in history, there are times when they serve the purpose well, and events follow along smoothly. At other times, inner conflicts surface, leading to uncertainty and confusion. Even in the best of times, however, the ways of knowing that any given culture develops inevitably establish certain limits and restrictions. People see the world from one particular perspective, and they ignore or fail to notice what does not match that point of view.

In our time, we can see for ourselves the result of these internal tensions. Even though Western

civilization has made a deep commitment to philosophy, science, psychology, religion, and other
styles of knowing, obstacles and difficulties still
arise. Individuals experience distractions, disap-
pointments, and disillusionment. Even the most
highly developed ways of knowing do not give us
the ability to solve our problems or to understand
our internal thoughts, feelings, and emotions. They
do not guarantee that we will be able to transform
or transcend our usual ways of operating the mind,
even when we can see for ourselves the difficulties
that result.

For the past several years, I have been reflecting on
this situation, asking myself how we can take a few
steps forward—how we can develop new ways of
thinking and understanding. Buddhist teachings
offer important guidance, and there are practices
that can help us engage our minds and thoughts
in new ways. When we do so, we strengthen our
own innermost core, coming closer to the root of
our existence.

In the outer world, events ripple through time,
manifesting at the level of society, the environment,
and events of all kinds. But inwardly, the mind gen-
erates ripples that shape our experience in a more
fundamental way.

At present, we are caught in certain ways of using the mind, bound by language and concepts that we cannot pass beyond. If we could change such fundamental patterns, we might be able to advance our own understanding. We might even find it possible to create the conditions for transforming the difficulties we now encounter.

In writing these essays, it has not been my intention to undermine or criticize more traditional forms of knowledge such as science or religion. Instead, my sense is that we can develop a way of knowing that cooperates with the intrinsic nature of mind, allowing more light to shine, accommodating our ordinary thoughts and ways of seeing while allowing them to function in more open ways. The potential benefit is great, for if we can make friends with the mind, we can embody a way of being that makes our lives meaningful and gives purpose to our time on earth.

Few people know very much about how to use the mind. It is constantly running off in all directions, like a herd of wild horses. Yet it does not take that much to develop a more cooperative way of engaging awareness. When body, mind, and thoughts come into harmony, we can find ourselves on a unique journey. Cultivating our own capacities, we can direct the mind in fruitful ways, achieving our highest goals and taking a profit from being alive. We can accommodate understanding and support the lineage of knowledge. We can discover for ourselves why we are here and where we are going next. Our journey through life can become rich in significance.

When our lives become richer, we find meaning in all that we do and all that we encounter. Even the obstacles that arise and the residues of negativity that bubble up can become resources for the journey. Step by step, we can climb the ladder that leads toward transformation and transcendence.

If these essays seem hard at times to grasp, please do not be discouraged. Just as scarecrows protect the crops in the field, so the shadows we encounter, the places we do not understand, play a useful role. They show us how the mind tends to turn away from knowledge, and toward distraction. They reveal the destructive patterns in which the mind can get trapped, and the dangers that can come with misunderstanding.

These are the patterns of our own mind. If we can approach them as friends, we might find them surprisingly open, generous, and accommodating.

As long we do not embody knowledge, we move through life as if we were lost or asleep. We would like to do it differently. We would like to develop ways of cooperating with the mind; we would like to create a new home for awareness.

Let yourself be open, set aside your skepticism about what is possible, and see for yourself what benefits may come.

Going

"Be here now." It sounds simple. But how did we get here, and how do we stay here? Could we have gotten here without taking some sort of path?

Certainly our lives have contained all kinds of events, some we don't clearly recall, some we remember vividly. It seems necessary for any 'now' to have a past which serves as its basis. From actions to concepts, from history to language, our experience is rooted in the past; without the past, we could not position ourselves in the present.

Each discipline has a different way of looking at it and explaining it. But ultimately, however we get here, we arrive. Presumably everything that happens to me happens here, and now: this is where reality is, at least for me.

But it seems to me there is room to question. How do I know I am here, and now? Do I really remember the steps that brought me here?

I know about my journey, for my mind, I am sure, recorded it; I know I arrived. Arrival and knowing about arrival, in fact, seem to be linked. But how did we get to 'now' from the past, and according to what steps?

And do we really know what 'now' means?

If we look at our experience of time, particularly our sense of persisting in and moving through time, it would seem to require mind and body, working together, to get us from the past to the present.

On one side, we have the actions, the events—the changes that take place over time. On the other side, we have our recollection of these events. These two facets of experience have a momentum of their own, as actions are sorted into coherent memories by the mind. It gives our movement through time a gait, as if we walked from the past to the present. One leg would be my mind with its set of memories; the other one, all that occurs, the force of those actions I took somehow driving me forward.

Experience goes along this way, shifting weight or emphasis from one side to the other, from memory to action and back. With these two legs, I walk, eventually reaching a place I call 'now.'

The way we walk has implications for our journey.

Rotating in this way between memory and action sets us up with sequences, consequences… causes. The mind notices that steps follow, one upon the other. It notices the sequence and makes inferences about it, inferences that guide our walking. The recording mind, tracking changes, creates the causal framework by which we understand experience.

Why should I be concerned about this, these causal chains I create as I walk? This is, surely, what anyone does. But when we begin to look at this activity, body and mind loping together across time, it might afford us a chance to ask deeper questions about what our sequences have set up for us to be and do.

Consider the rhythm, the cadence of this walking. Step by step, things occur; one by one, I notice them, I remember. My mind records what occurred, feeds it back to memory, where other events, other occurrences, seem to be stored.

It's true that a lot has happened; maybe I lost a few parts, failed to track every detail, but I can reconstruct the journey around the gaps in my memory. Step by step, I arrived: I reached the point of the present.

But I can't help but wonder: before these gaps crept into my memory, how did my experiences get recorded, so they could show up as experience? What if we took a look at the recording, caught it in the midst of its work, after the end of one snapshot in time, and before the beginning of the next?

The recorder records what occurs. Each step would seem to be recorded, but the recording process itself, which surely must have its own beginning, middle, and end, is murky. When and how the recording is made—the point when the photographer takes the picture—is not clear.

That inspires me to ask certain questions.

* How does the recorder actually register events?

* Is the recording activity simultaneous with the recorded event? Is there any kind of gap between them?

* Is the recording of an event the same thing as the recollection of an event? Is the recorder the

same as the rememberer? Or is the rememberer in the present, while the recorder is in the past?

How did the beginning, middle, and conclusion get recorded? Understanding this could have real ramifications for experience, if we stop to consider the character of the conclusions we often come to about our experience. Our conclusions—our 'happy', 'sad', or 'disappointed'—have a *conclusive* effect on the quality of our lives.

Who drew these conclusions on our behalf?

Is it possible that this memorizing photographer is not the same person as the one who actually had the experience? And is the photographer the same as me, right now? Are we, somehow, three? Or more than three: Is the photographer the same as the person who picks up the finished images?

In other words, is the 'one who' was observing the experience and recorded it, so to speak, the same as the one who observes the recorded memory? At that moment, the recorder-mind might be operating in the past tense, and in the present, is nowhere to be found.

When the snapshot is taken, am I in the picture at all, or is the photographer taking a selfie?

I might say "I am of two minds," but really, I don't think I believe that idea; we don't take such sayings literally. I am one; I feel like one; at any rate, I feel certain that my mind is not dividable; at any rate, it's been solid, up to now.

But then, if that were true, how could I take these steps? Walking takes two legs; similarly, getting to the present moment seems to require both gestures, both parts, body and mind. Action is not the same as memory.

They seem different; but if they were to stop moving, one after the other in turn, action and memory, left and right, the momentum of our experience would fall apart. If there is any consistency to what we call 'being here now,' it seems we need both actions to occur, and that means that something has to differ from itself, in order to rotate.

At the same time, in the momentum of our transit, some properties clearly have to be shared across this divide. We don't know how that sharing between the two sides takes place. But it seems they must be connected.

Something is happening 'now'; something is pointing out and being pointed out, reflecting and reflected. These reflections, feeding back, are downloaded into experience—reflections that coexist as the photographer, the coordinator of experience, and perhaps even the picture itself.

I carry on, ever departing, ever arriving in that place, my place, in 'now'—and that continuous momentum sends me forward, to the next experience. And the next, and the next, and the next…

I: Well, yes. That is my journey.

Mind: Do you know much about this journey you call *yours*?

I: … I can't say that I do.

We believe there is a forward momentum to events, to thoughts and experiences. We don't really know how anything could go, other than forward. Maybe there could be another way, but we don't know what that other direction's basis could be, or what momentum it could possibly have. As far as we can tell, everything goes 'to'. That's our orientation, our direction.

That's our *instruction*. We know how to obey that order: we're all too good at taking direction.

This walk we take—this journey—affects everything we are.

Subject expressions, like 'me', or 'you', shape our understanding. Language has that kind of power over experience; and it feeds back directly to history, to our own life story, and the life stories of everyone else. But all of it depends on something; it's not just standing there by itself. It all depends on judgments, on values, on the characters and qualities we give things; it all depends on memory, mind, and action, those three coordinators who urgently need to be coordinated, themselves.

How do they get coordinated? How does meaning emerge from this activity? If we could change the conclusions, perhaps we could change the terms of engagement of our problems. We could transform the meanings, and meaning could make us something new.

These questions may seem strange, abstract, distant from real life—but they speak directly to the texture of experience itself. If we could understand this, we would suddenly have a choice, a choice that's nothing like the painful forced choices of the samsaric regime.

The benefit would be enormous, not just to us, but to everyone with whom we interact, rolling out in bigger and bigger ripples from our individual lives. We could make a paradise out of here and now.

It is even possible that we could discover how to pick the locks of universal suffering, *sarvam dukkham*, and learn enough about its operation to reverse samsara, all of it—all that ubiquitous and permanent misery.

That's why I care about this: because we deserve to have a better journey.

We sentient beings, dropped into the middle of our own experience, almost never get to ask how it all began. We never get a say in where it all goes. We pick up our models, assume our continuity, play our parts—and it all goes along as if it's on wheels, with an automatic transmission.

And doing that means being good. 'Being good' means we have completed our education. We are all grown up: we know how to transmit reality.

Today, as a part of samsara's inevitable pull, or possibly the specific material orientations of Western science, or just collective bad karma, it is hard to make contact with knowledge that is not entirely structured by discrimination: the dividing of our experience by a perceiving and judging awareness.

When we look behind the concepts that make up our knowledge we find no light: only loops, an astounding number of tight, compressed loops, the feedbacks of sense and perception. These sensory products of mind are plugged into the conceptual apparatus; they found and ground and are themselves authorized by its insistence, in vicious circles of 'reasons' and 'evidence.'

Lacking real solutions, real wisdom, we more or less conclude that freedom is not possible—not at the present time.

Not at this moment.

> I: But that's not good enough! We have a serious problem here. How do we fix it?

> **Mind:** 'How', indeed.

We are fortunate to inhabit the global culture of the twenty-first century; we have formidable technical knowledge, and access to vast archives of recorded, interpreted experience. Yet we possess close to no examples, no models, and no teachers who could help us take a different path.

Deprived of all other skillful means, bereft of any training in the methods of transformation, our only vehicle is 'how'.

'How' is how we gather knowledge. 'How' determines what courses of action we may take. 'How' assumes the present parameters are real and must be obeyed. How else could we do it?

Held hostage by our own 'how', we may begin to despair. The vision of freedom, of a different kind of knowledge, may start to seem a little like Western concepts of Heaven: beautiful, desirable, and a long way off.

Even if we use Sanskrit terms like 'Prajna', or reach for words in our own languages that mean 'wisdom', or 'higher knowledge', or 'emptiness', or 'enlightenment', we find that our meanings still occupy a precinct that was set up in advance. All of these concepts, no matter how inspiring and uplifting, are conditioned by what we presently know.

For us, getting answers means having conceptual thoughts—nothing more or less. We are only partially aware of the deep decision-making involved

when mind endorses the meaning of those labels...
and only partially aware of the cost.

With our 'how' we howl for our freedom, lonely
wolves howling at a distant moon.

> I: I couldn't do it. I read about the regime of
> mind, I learned about the problems, I tried
> to answer the questions, I did. But I couldn't
> get anywhere different. I guess I'm just stuck
> here.
>
> **Me**: This always happens to me.
>
> I: I'm tired of thinking about it.
>
> **Me**: Hey... Maybe there's a snack for me in
> the kitchen.
>
> I [sighing]: Right. What's the point?

The point is...

The point is that all of us, every lonely traveler who
has ever lived and struggled, whose experience unfolds in time: all of us need help. Our future is at
stake here. We deserve better than this.

The point is, we have an opportunity to learn something truly new. Can we travel a different road?

This is not an idle question. Our inquiry is not just of theoretical or philosophical interest. If there is even a chance that we could change the character of our being in time, what doors might open to us?

The sequential way our lives work is interesting, and worth exploring. This is our own precious, irreplaceable, lived experience. More than any ancient teaching, any book, our experience has the potential to offer us great knowledge, and the possibility of real growth. If we could understand how it all operates, we could become real creators. Real creators, and *real* creators: creators of our own reality.

Chapter Two:
Knowing

Introduction to Chapter Two

The purpose of these essays is to promote under-standing of the meanings of the regime of mind. All of us trapped in samsara are under the control of mind's regime. Following its rule, acting on its behalf, we accept the situation we are in, and we form our concepts accordingly.

To free ourselves from the regime of mind, the first step is to know clearly what the real situation is. The second step is to understand the operations of the regime. The third step is to discover how we can enter a realm of freedom, where a meaning beyond meanings plays.

If we look first at the situation we presently inhabit, we could say that the regime of mind is active in all directions, surrounding us like the circumfer-ence of a circle. In the east is awareness; in the west is consciousness, with its capacity to remind us of the way things are. In the south are the activities of mind: temptations, the exhibitions of the sensory fields, the busy-ness of minding, and all kinds of distractions. In the north are the spies who make sure all is proceeding according to plan, as well as the ones who dictate the rules we follow.

Living within the environment marked out in this way, we take the same actions again and again. The momentum of time sweeps us up. It points out and interprets, establishes meanings and dictates what is so, and labels each arising perception. Ruled by the kleshas, surrounded 360 degrees, we are caught in guilt trips and toxic emotionality that serve to reinforce the regime. There is nowhere else to go, no possible escape. In each direction, we are completely captured.

Our responsibility is to build up an understanding of these dimensions of our experience and their consequences for our lives. We need to be clear about the distractions that rob us of awareness and the emotionality that manifests in karma and klesha. We need to acknowledge the feelings we experience, the truths we assert, our bondage to pleasure and pain, our obsessions, our experience of loneliness and guilt, Not knowing our origins or our destiny, ignorant of the DNA of our existence or the future that sentient beings face, we must be clear about the momentum that drives the workings of samsara, the cause and effect determinations that leave us with no other options.

In spelling out these patterns, we are not engaging in scare tactics, nor are we saying that we must find *a way out*, another 'place' to go. What we are asking is how we can learn to operate differently within the regime of mind—going behind each point, opening new spaces and new places. There are treasures we have lost, but we can recover them.

How can we speak of these possibilities? In ancient times people spoke of magical kingdoms. In Christianity Jesus speaks of a kingdom that is not of this earth. The Buddha spoke of the heaven realms, and Guru Padmasambhava simply spoke of bliss. The Bodhisattvas speak of Great Love, and the Dharma speaks of leaving behind samsara by following the path that leads to self-liberation. These are the ways that tradition has proclaimed.

My sense is that such descriptions, whether we think of them as historical or as existing only in the imagination, are not relevant to modern times. They are too easily dismissed as legend. I want to bring such possibilities close to us, as close as our hearts. I want people to realize that human knowledge has the capacity to provide what we need; that we can rely on our own understanding to free ourselves from the dictatorship of suffering; that we can choose to liberate ourselves.

Knowing

In our ordinary understanding, knowing always seems to know *something*.

Even though we have learned a lot about the self-image, and a lot about the painful effects of objectification on the world we live in, we should not underestimate the power of the subject-object set-up: it is so deeply ingrained, so reflexive, that if the first half of the equation is present, the other half may also be operating—out in the open, or in a hidden way.

When knowers are present, keep an eye out for 'things to know'.

When objects are present, keep an eye out for the ones who look for objects.

We are so well-schooled in this doctrine that even our attempts to describe a knowing beyond subjects and objects very often founder on things to know… and the implacable desire to know.

Knowing knows... but how?

I've been wondering.

Presumably, in order to be known, things must occur.

Not just the things that appear to our senses, but all things, including memories, thoughts, concepts, values, and judgments. We call this arising 'truth', or 'experience', or 'reality'. Things, thoughts of things, and thoughts of thoughts: all the equipment and apparatus of regime.

All of these arise in time, mysteriously; all of these are made up of points pointed out, in layers and layers of patterned perception, unfolding in time, time after time. Produced by and according to rhythms of time, the layers shift and move like ripples, gradually gathering force.

This set-up sets up our situations. Not only our personal dramas, the pain and discomfort of our particular lives, but the main frameworks that let those dramas take place: The subject and its orientation. The object and its presentation. The feedback of object to subject... and vice versa.

"I see it": from this seeing comes many things. Or possibly everything: everything we call objective, everything we call subjective, real things and unreal things and all the commentaries and evaluations that take these things for their object: in fact, an entire apparatus of reasoning.

In order to be *known*, things must be *shown*.

If an object never showed up to a subject, if 'I' never saw 'it', it is unclear how any of this could be established.

But what about this object? How does it appear to me? What presents the object to the subject, and how is it done? Is this presentation related in any way to time?

These may not be questions we normally feel free to ask. But when we have a chance to contemplate quietly, we might begin to notice some things about noticing things.

If there is something 'shown', then the knowable is known: we are sure it must be there.

But where?

In order to appear, it seems the object must present itself at some *point*. If a means for differentiating times is not there, if time is not divided into times, can anything actually appear?

Let's imagine that something shows up, at a point we call 'present'. To exist, this thing would need to have some kind of duration, even if only a very short one. There must be some occupancy of time, and of times: something that went on in the past, goes on now, and keeps going on into the future.

If I'm going to say that something's there, then it needs to persist, moment by moment. It seems that things need a bridge of some kind to get them across time. But is there any possible bridge here? The bridge must connect the times that were separate; but what about the space between the bridging links, the space that would be necessary in order to differentiate the bridge from what it bridges?

The bridge would have to remain distinct from the times it connects. If this hypothetical bridge were built from time itself, past time or present time or future time, then we would still encounter a gap, a space, when the past-time-bridge ended and the present moment began. It seems we would need a bridge—another bridge—to bridge the gaps between the bridges themselves, and the past, present and future.

We could try to avoid this problem by imagining a bridge that was not part of time. But if the bridge between times were somehow built of something other than time, there would still be a gap, a difference, between the bridges and the times being bridged. How are the things we know conducted over these gaps? Do they disappear and then reappear? How do we know they are the same objects in each time?

Without segmented time, the object could not present itself to the subject; there would be no present moment that would permit it to emerge into being. It seems that either everything would always already have to be here, or else, nothing whatsoever could come into existence—for if time is a continuum with no distinct past, present, or future, there can be no moment of arising.

On the other hand, if time is truly dividable into coherent, distinct times—like the cars of a train—

it is not clear what connects the train cars together into continuity. Without this continuity, where can our objects reside? At what point in time are they pointed out?

But this makes it seem as if nothing could possibly appear to view—nothing recognizable. And we know our experience is full of 'knowables', objects and states we can identify.

Our things must be here: somehow they must have arrived. We can bear witness to their showing—after all, we pointed them out.

We feel this showing and knowing must have been going on for a long time—as long as we can remember. The longer it goes on, in fact, the more secure it seems as a way of knowing. My own pointing action makes me feel certain that I saw something at some point. I feel sure…or at least, I want to feel sure. I need to feel sure.

I'm longing to be sure.

And the longer showing and knowing goes on, the longer the longer goes on longing. Someone needs that object to appear. This longing may have a part to play in what is shown and known, as showing and knowing feed back to themselves.

Insofar as everything I am can be articulated as a set of identifiable properties, I depend on what is mine. And what is mine is precisely what is at stake, when we look more closely at time.

It is powerful magic, the magic of time and sequence. First, second, and third; past, present, future: these make our reality. But time, which fosters every aspect of our being human, seems to be a strange and tricky guardian. Past, present and future do not seem to carry our objects along.

And our own longing for belonging: how does it persist?

Perhaps I could just ignore my problems with past and future, and not worry about if they support me now. The most important point, after all, is the present. Isn't that where I'm standing? But without future, without past, how can I have that present, as *presently* understood?

We have seen that the past supports the present; it is the source of all patterning, and it permits us to recognize what we see. But the future, too, plays a critical role. For all our experience was once sup-posedly the future. In the past, the present was the future; consider what happens to experience if we have no projected future whatsoever! Without an expectation of futurity, life runs off a cliff.

At the same time, our way of understanding the fu-ture is profoundly modeled on the experiences of the past. *Will be, will do:* these are based on past patterning. An extrapolation from the past might keep *presenting* the past, the light from lost stars il-luminating our next moment, and our next—each 'next' a perfect copy of the last 'next'.

Somehow, the *known* was *shown.*

But we can't seem to pin down the moment of knowing.

With this, we may have come to a point where we don't feel able to continue; we are too puzzled. We can at least say that about the situation—we don't understand, we don't know where to go, we are puzzled.

But our puzzle is not reliable, the way we feel our objects are reliable. There is something fragmentary about a puzzle. It may contain an assemblage of points—points of perception, or points of thought, intuition or feeling—but we cannot identify the thing the points represent. The outline is incomplete, or the internal contradictions are too severe. "I am puzzled" is our conclusion. We put the lid back on the box; we shelve the case as 'unsolved'.

But this conclusion is a fake. It's a mirage, like a scarecrow, a mock-up that's put up to scare off scavengers. The refuge it provides is temporary.

It seems to give me a position, a place to be: puzzled. I have to take that position, since I have no solutions. But this is not a stable place to stand. Instead I find myself wandering, wondering. My questions have run out of answers, so I take to the road, my thoughts driven off, away from the unknown.

I give up on further inquiry, scared by my own scarecrow.

In order to recognize reality, I need an object: then I can be 'objective'. My subjectivity depends on it. But the object's 'that-ness', rapidly pointed out by mind, may also be a kind of scarecrow.

The zigzag movement of questions and answers sets up a rhythm: back to the subject, forward to the conclusion, the object, and back again.

Both poles of the movement depend on 'is', manufactured by language and sealed by the mind. But 'is', in turn, may be little more than a product of this restless movement from seer to seen and back again. Self-reinforced and self-reinforcing, 'is' might *be* this loop, mind's movement's manufacture.

'Is' has inertia. Once 'is' is set up, I can only follow along in accord with what language says, what mind endorses.

Mind: Take a memo: take this dictation on behalf of mine, I, self.

I: In the manner of an "I"?

Mind: Correct.

I: All right, I'll begin.

Mind: The recommendation is as follows… are you writing this down?

I: Yes, sir, I am.

In our world, knowing quickly becomes knowledge, a *shown known*.

The kingdom of knowledge contains abundant treasure. But this treasure may have limits. I have knowledge, but I need more; I need antidotes, solutions. For each piece of knowledge is ambivalent; and sometimes the cure is worse than the disease.

What can I do about this? There is nothing to do except keep looking, keep adding to the supply. I must keep digging in my 'mine.'

When knowing becomes *something to know*, then I must go seek it out.

Wall, nest, trap; I, mine, mind; my knowledge, my scarecrow: these things arise through and depend on dualities. They are the product of mental projections, points and responses to points. This is knowing, according to all my best information. This is my long wander, point to point to point.

Is it possible to penetrate the loop?

'I' requires its experience—its body, senses, and view; its tools, ideas, way of thinking, and projections. "I" needs to make its things secure, and "I" needs these things to make itself secure.

This is its viewpoint; and its objects, themselves, are view-*points*, productions of pointing.

But to whom, or to what, does knowing belong? We cannot easily assign knowing to the subject side or the object side. Yet we also cannot do away with or do without knowing: all our points have been produced by knowing.

So at what point does knowing occur? If I point to a point called 'the point of knowing', is knowing found at that point? Or in the pointing?

Westerners place a high value on knowledge that comes 'from' someone, someone who knows. I learn, I receive, 'from' that someone. But there might be an internal knowing that does not participate in 'from' and 'to'.

It seems that all potential understanding is mine; on the other hand, maybe there can be no 'mine' to knowledge.

Beyond the loop, in the heart of time where know-ing resides, knowledge may be free as air.

Identities seem to take shape as signals shine out, shuttling sensing down dualistic tunnels, and into corrals, concepts, and structures. But at the point of application, the point where, supposedly, all ex-perience finds its feet, we may not be able to place objects, or identify subjects.

If we could understand the way all this operates— how our sense of being, of knowing, gives rise to the real—perhaps we could discern how sensing accommodates manifestation. And once we under-stood sensing, that fresh air might be there for us to breathe freely. Knowing in time may render all knowledge translucent; for it seems at the heart of time, the entire edifice is shimmering.

What is knowledge at this moment, this un-point-able point? If knowing knows no borders, it cannot be located, limited, or measured. Never created or discovered, it cannot ever be lost.

Going beyond these instrumental operations we have been taught to call 'inquiry' brings us to the shores of a new ocean. It is not about looking at a picture. The realization, the revelation, and the recognition are together. Seeing, being, and doing are one.

The discovery of the nature of mind may be nothing other than the operation of knowing beyond all grammar.

And in the end, 'showing' and 'shining' may have much in common.

Chapter Three: Ruling

Introduction to Chapter Three

As we begin to engage the possibilities that appear when we study the operations of mind, there is reason to be cautious. An intellectual understanding of these ideas could cause us to grow a little disdainful of the rules and roles, the positions and possessions that structure our experience. 'After all', we may rationalize, 'they are not really real'.

But even this attitude of disrespect bears the marks of our entrapment in the mirage. For 'not-real' itself, as a category, is entirely dependent on the real as a 'real' thing that can be distinguished from everything else.

Without the real standing in the background, a phrase like "it's not real" makes no sense at all.

In order to avoid getting stuck in the oppositions that organize our concepts and ideas, we will need to take an approach that is at the same time more gentle and forgiving of the mirage, and more careful and aware of its pervasiveness and depth.

For in fact, as we become more alert to the operations of mind, we cannot help but notice that these essays, in order to communicate new insights, *themselves* present concepts and make use of the ingredients and products generated by our language-enchanted minds.

Loosening the yoke of language is not a simple matter: we cannot just abandon words, images and perceptions in search of a 'really real' beneath or behind our structures. Even the idea of such abandonment puts us back inside the enclosure of ordinary mind, with its careful distinctions between good and bad, relevant and irrelevant, true and false; it puts us back within the purview of the enchanted mind's insistence on a method or a course of action, a 'how-to' that will solve the problem of the mind's mirages once and for all.

Inevitably we project such concepts; without 'how', we have no idea how it can be done. Models for operating the mind differently are very scarce, and may not yet exist in the Western world. In fact, when we encounter testaments to other possibilities, we human beings have a propensity to translate them back into the terms with which we are familiar.

We can see the consequences of this entrapment fairly clearly when we consider the way important

Buddhist concepts like *shunyata* have been received in the West.

Shunyata is the heart of Prajnaparamita, the Buddha's transcendent wisdom that penetrates the nature of form. *Prajna,* or wisdom, is the full flowering of the process of understanding *shunyata.*

This understanding can take a very long time to achieve. *Shunyata* is a deep and difficult subject, not one that can be casually accounted for and encompassed in concepts and words.

According to the currently accepted translations, *shunyata* means something akin to 'emptiness.' But this translation is preliminary at best, and raises many questions.

Language's labels present us with a tableau of rules and roles, tightly bounded by the unknown. Even words like 'wisdom', 'transcendent' or 'beyond' cannot get us very far. We may not notice that a term like 'beyond' itself depends upon a pointer, someone whose 'here' and 'there' determine the extent of knowledge, and whose horizon is strictly limited. 'Beyond' does not seem to have gotten us beyond the concept's limit.

These restricted orientations are not solely the province of Western minds, but we can see them play out in Western meanings when terms like *shunyata* are translated. 'Emptiness', often chosen as an English word for *shunyata,* is a term that functions within a paradigm of *things*—things that are perceived as really existing, and whose negation produces emptiness.

But *the opposite of 'things being present'* may not be an adequate translation of *shunyata.*

We may never become fully aware of how much pressure our paradigms place on the mind's ability to understand. These are the ordinary building-blocks by which we construct our picture of the world, but they are also deeply constraining assumptions that may not, in the end, apply to the *operator* of the operations of mind.

So far, Western attempts to understand Prajna-paramita seem to rely heavily on the creation and interpretation of concepts, and on clever, paradoxical playing with words. English as a Dharma vehicle has flexibility and a certain potential, but it may not yet possess the means by which to translate terms like *shunyata* or *prajna.* Much more groundwork will be needed to find ways to communicate the knowledge of Prajnaparamita successfully.

I cannot overstate the challenge this situation presents. Understanding cannot be cultivated through study alone; practice is required, and a serious, consistent engagement with the *not-knowing* engendered by language, as it marks the manifestations of mind.

I want to encourage you to work your way slowly and patiently through these ideas, and not to reject them when they become difficult. Indeed, we are not in the business of rejecting anything, not even the samsaric structures of mind. Instead, we seek to know them better; to discern, with greater and greater clarity, the force they exert on freedom.

Let us do our best to learn everything we can, exploring not only *everything*, but *we* and *can* as well.

Ruling

In order to create architecture, we need engineering, blueprints, a plan. Similarly, in order to create new shapes and forms of culture, new ways of being and seeing, we will need some conceptual clarity about the engineering of our experience.

In the past this clarity may have been a little hard to come by, but we have the power, within our own experience, to make new shapes and forms: we can make the rest of our journey something creative and meaningful.

In many respects, this journey seems to depend on our identity, the productions we have called 'I', 'me', and 'mine'.

These productions, in their turn, require the mind's full faith and confidence in their meaning. They need to be endorsed, accepted as real, in order to function.

Their realness, their real–*ness*, anchors experience.

The world of matter may ultimately emerge from space, yet the things I see and deal with have shape and form. In the same way, mind creates its designs, bodying forth myriad shapes and forms out of its potential.

It starts with the most primitive products of mind, manifested through our sense faculties, our pattern-matching ability, and our subconscious. Gradually, our perceptions are consolidated into projections, entities... identities. As the layers get laid down, they are located in space and time; rules are elaborated, policies established—an entire constitution to govern the territories of mind.

Some of its components are presented by language. Some of them may precede denotative, propositional language, incubated in the feedback loops of sense perceptions, the call-and-response of stimulus and reaction.

The rules, roles, and forms, and how to make them manifest, all of this is projected and sustained by mind: all the doctrines and all the schools, all the

feedbacks of all the loops of cognized and cognizing consciousness.

Mind is the one who set up 'I' and 'me', who devised
the plan and wrote the constitution, who compiles
the sensations, the perceptions, and the ideas. Mind
is the holder of experience, coordinator of 'what I
know'; mind is the means by which what is known
and the 'I' who knows form their unity.

Mind manifests I: *now I'm real.*

Mind says 'yes' to I, to me, to mine: mind endorses
the manifestations of mind. Mind's rules compose
a grid in which space allows forms to manifest, and
time allows experience to manifest, so that different
situations arise and pass away.

Positions and possessions established, the mind,
like a good stage manager, incessantly puts on productions based on its grid; and senses, body positions, rhythms of time experience, and interpretations of language concepts all contribute, playing
their parts.

Time is a key part of this theater. Time's energy manifests mind's activity, its rhythms constellating experience, moving us from Point A to Point B. Or maybe we should say, from Point A to Point 'I', from Point B to Point 'Me', and from Point C to Point 'Mind'.

But how does this work? Is experience moving? Are these points present, in space or time? We may be able to say that we are 'here and now'—we may know how to use those words in a sentence—but experientially, we may not actually be able to recognize anything we could call a present point, the point-dimension of the singularity of our pointing.

How, then, is experience actually unfolding over time? If there is no reliable information, no knowledge about our experience, we cannot pin it down.

And if we cannot pin it down, there may be some significant consequences for our journey.

A certain 'ness' seems to be the key ingredient that gives continuity to our experience in time. The sky's colors may change, but the sky reliably remains the sky; it has 'sky-ness'.

That 'ness', traveling from past to present to future, from Point 'I' to Point 'Me', gives me my steadiness over time; it gives my experience its solidity and diversity, its 'is-ness'.

Every conceivable thing, from flowers to stars, seems to possess this 'is-ness'; otherwise, it could not be identified as something distinct from everything else. Every shifting tone or turn of mind, too, has its character, its 'ness'. Perhaps we could think of having 'ness' as the Rule: it determines what is, and keeps the set-up straight. In fact, this Rule permits all our rules to come into being; it is a precondition of all ruling.

The Rule is not a minor or contingent part of experience; it anchors our recognition of ourselves as beings in time. That being, permitted according to the Rule, seems to be the heart of the matter, a precious element that is transmitted, step by step, to the present of being.

But the question of how—or whether—time-instants are actually coordinated in a sequence has a material impact on whether the conventional account of experience can be trusted; and this, in turn, has an impact on whether the Rule upon which we rely can be constituted.

According to our ordinary picture of experience,

1.   Time is linear.

2.   Time is segmented; past, present, and future can be distinguished from one another.

3.   Experience has movement; it flows from past, to present, and into the future, three moments that can be differentiated and categorized as coherent parts of time.

Yet each instant in the continuity, if we look at it closely, has an odd quality of past-ness about it. As soon as it is recognized, as soon as it occupies a point to which we can point, it is no longer present. It becomes very tricky to figure out how to pin down any of the points of our conventional model of lived time as they occur. The act of placing a pin in the present moment seems to send it into the past; we miss the target every time.

Our rules seem to require moments in which to appear. But the Rule of 'ness' may not actually be operating in the present moment.

If we cannot point to the present, point it out, what are the implications for what we call real? For ruling seems to depend on pointing; and the Rule anchors the pointedness of the point.

Can we have the Rule of 'ness' without pointing out its products?

If we cannot, what does that imply about the manifested products of mind?

In order to make myself secure, I need to make sure of what has occurred to mind. I need experience to have shape and form. I need to be able to coordinate, to operate according to the concept of the construction. If I can't fulfil these conditions, it's not clear that I can maintain my consistency.

We are so certain of these structures, 'I' and 'me', 'mine' and 'mind'! But without the 'nesses' of experience, how could they operate? That is the real question.

The question becomes especially relevant when we reflect on the nature of so many of our 'nesses'—the anger, frustration and loneliness in which we so often live. These 'nesses' seem to be architecting the suffering we endure ourselves, and witness in our loved ones.

It may take a little stretching to see the operation of the Rule more clearly. But when we seek to understand in a way that moves beyond the precinct of our ordinary concepts, the inertial power of our 'nesses' becomes more apparent.

Consider our attempts to communicate and understand emptiness. For most of us, a word like *shunyata* is something to hold onto. The word gives us a meaning, a concept we can grasp. This meaning lets *shunyata* operate in a world of subjects and objects; it lets *shunyata* belong to the mind.

This meaning participates in a system of meanings: meanings that can be categorized as 'subjective' or 'objective'—as fields of feeling, or equations.

As experiencers, we dwell in the fields of feeling made possible by meaning. But how do the supposedly objective aspects of our system of meanings operate? In what sense should we call these 'objective' meanings equations?

We could say that an equation's purpose is to capture points; it is designed to delineate the territories of mind.

Equations, correctly solved, 'zero out'—they leave no remainder. Or to put it another way, the remainder of the equation is nothing less than 'nothing remains'.

What is that 'nothing' that remains? Is it a quality? A potential? A comparison? A non-description of an indescribable pointing-out?

The 'nothing' created here has its own 'ness'; it is nothing other than a something that's been cut out, removed. We could say that insofar as equations 'zero out', what equations produce as a byproduct of their being solved is zero as a graspable concept.

The Rule that distinguishes thing from thing could be seen as an equation or formula in this sense, for it provides for the possibility of all characterizable experience.

That said, the Rule itself may not point to any real essence or thing. Instead, it permits meanings to mean. It supports the implicit comparisons and differentiations that hide inside any given meaning and allow it to mean 'this' and 'not that'.

Words function by staging implicit comparisons of terms; 'red' contains a rainbow of foreclosed colors, colors we rule out when we look at 'red'. In the sense that words contain such comparisons, we could characterize them as *ratios*.

We could say that the Rule of 'ness' functions a little like the bar or line that separates the terms in such a ratio. It has no contents, no positive identity whatsoever; like the bar of a ratio, it is a cut, a dividing stroke: a negation.

Mind creates its architecture—its habitable forms of thought—using ratios, comparisons, rhythms. All of these depend on negation's cut, on the ability to distinguish 'this' from 'not this'. Each of our identifications is a product of such a cut. Empty of meaning—empty even of essence—the Rule permits essence, as it permits all taxonomy, all the sorting, paring, distinguishing activities of mind.

According to our assumptions, inculcated in us by our education, this is how thinking works: it deals with objects, arranged in a space that has been staked out and declared empty. Against this backdrop, things stand out; without their backdrop, they could not be recognized.

Without these out-standing things, without the backdrop that shows the things to us, how could we do thinking? If there are no cuts, there are no things, and the project of thinking simply collapses: it falls into a nihilism in which subject and object are both lost, foreclosed.

Therefore, we conclude, thinking against its backdrop must proceed, business as usual; the project must go forward.

Words like *shunyata* function for us in precisely this way. Meditators remind themselves: "Nothing has to be prevented or accommodated." Meanwhile, something, some *nothing*, guides and gives rise to these inactions.

Any identifiable existent thing has been vacuumed out; the vacuum remains.

The Rule has been executed. The equation has zeroed out: We have solved for 'ness'.

The mind's cut is not a timeless distinction, an activity taking place in the abstract. In fact, this cut is distinctly timed.

When the cut occurs, something mysterious happens: the products of experience, its recognizable elements appear right away, fully delineated. The cut instantly produces 'up' and 'down', 'male' and 'female'—even 'clear' and 'unclear'.

It seems there is a temporality involved, a 'before the cut' and an 'after the cut'. Before the cut, the products 'clear' and 'unclear' could not be distinguished by the mind. After the cut, 'clear' and 'unclear' are as obvious and different as night and day. And when we look at them, the states called 'before the cut' and 'after the cut' are similarly easy to tell apart.

If we look closely, however, we will notice that both of these states can only be distinguished by means of a cut. That means that even our 'before the cut' and 'after the cut' imply a cut that has already taken place.

The 'finished up', 'already happened' character of the cut makes identification of experience and allocation of labels possible. But when does the cut itself occur?

The cut of the mind that lets us tell our experiences apart, so that we can recognize the difference between 'this' and 'not this', must surely take place in some span of time, no matter how small. Presumably this cut has a beginning, middle, and end, for the products of mind cannot appear unless the cut itself is completed.

Time—a time with differences, with beginnings, middles, and ends—seems necessary in order to take any action. But the mind's cut—its Rule of negation—may be responsible for the delineations of time we experience.

Without the power to pass through, the sword of the mind cannot make a cut. But 'passing through', in distinguished, separated moments, would itself seem to be a product of the cutting action of mind.

That would suggest that without the cut, there is no way for the cut itself to begin or end.

So is the cut occurring? We say it has taken place, but did it ever *take place*?

If we cannot get this Rule firmly established—if we cannot work out a time-basis for the mind's cut—things may get a little strange.

The points of our experience seem positive to us—they've been with us awhile, and we recognize them. These 'things that are' are strongly conditioned by our sense that they are 'things that have been'. This sense of past-ness is what establishes them in our mind as *things*.

At the same time, the points of experience cannot be distinguished as points unless they have boundaries, unless they begin or end. If points are not unitary, it is not clear how they could serve as points. A unit should be unique; one point should be clearly distinguishable from its neighbors.

How is the difference established? How does negation's cut actually establish our points; and where do the cut-away points go? Without differentiated time there is no way for them to pass away, and make space for the next points.

But without cutting, there is no way for us to differentiate times.

Suddenly time is a collapsed bridge: we cannot cross over to the next instant of becoming.

What becomes of action? What becomes of experience? What becomes of our joy or sorrow, the rhythms and the patterns of our points? What becomes of the past, lost time of experience? If it is truly gone, how can the past become a memory or understanding? If it is truly gone, how does thinking carry on?

But if it is not gone, how can any given experience be articulated? Supposedly each point produces the point that follows; each point is a next-point-producer. If that is true, though, then maybe no point is ever fully past, never quite ending—or, by extension, beginning.

But this state of affairs would never allow our experience to take shape.

Past, present, and future seem to be projections, but at the same time, growth and change seem very real. Without points, we can have no rhythm or momentum forward. Without pointing out, how could there be any growth, change, or experience?

Without the palpable, authoritative grounding of 'experience', it is hard to prop up the structure of the self.

But without the Rule of 'nesses', experience as we understand it falls apart.

And without a point-able present, it is hard to establish the substantiality of any 'ness' at all.

This is very curious.

I: I… I must have a "before," and an "after." I must have this, you know, *this*—

Me: Can you point it out to me?

I: You know I can't!

Me: If time doesn't work the way we think, I wonder what's happening inside me… instead.

I: Don't be spooky.

Me: It *is* spooky.

Mind: *Is it?*

We seem to think that reality takes the form of *states*.

States are recognizable and distinctive. Ice is not the same as water, just as the United States is not Mexico. But in their difference from one another, states are not just more-than or less-than, not just operating in shifting ratios that describe their properties, depending on their neighbors. Instead, each state's distinct identity has been *ratified*, just as political states are ratified.

The mind accepts the presentation of the state as a done deal, thanks to the Rule, the negation of 'ness.' We are ruled by this Rule.

This can be a problem; for once states have been established, we can't do much with them. They are firmly held in place by their own past-ness. But if our 'nesses' have no intrinsic substance, perhaps we are less locked into states than we think. If the Rule is not really operating the way we think, what becomes of the power of the ruling regime?

Could we be free to walk away? Could we create something new?

Chapter Four:
Kingdom of Time

Introduction to Chapter Four

These essays could be thought of as a reading by mind, for mind, and to mind. They work with our ways of thinking and knowing, and they give us a way to direct our sense of knowing in a fruitful direction. However, they remain on a conceptual level, where language and words are in control. This means their impact is limited. When we stay at the level of the stories we know and the distinctions we can point out, we are still trying to understand the regime of mind through the 'bio-feedback' of mind projecting to mind. Eventually we need to find ways to go to a deeper level.

When we try to understand the operations of mind in an exclusively conceptual way, it is like trying to stir up the water in a still pool so that we can see our reflection more clearly. Our efforts only disturb the natural clarity of mind, and we see less than before. Introducing new ideas, asking new questions, and challenging accepted concepts can be valuable, but still, it will happen only rarely that the mind falls silent.

In part, the difficulty is that the mind that asks questions or wonders how knowing functions is still aiming to accomplish something. It wants to enjoy the fruits of inquiry, but this wish to get good results creates an internal tension. This is what churns up the still pool and obscures what might otherwise be clear. Observer mind, caught up in the entanglements of I and me and mine, cannot open the way for knowledge to emerge.

The same holds true in meditation. Beginners in meditation look for a place internally where they can feel at home, the way we like to have a comfortable chair in the corner of the living room. Of course, there are benefits to stimulating these kinds of positive feelings. It may encourage a sense of open appreciation and relaxation, and this can be a good first step. But this approach cannot transform karma and klesha.

When we practice in this way, we forget that the negative patterns of mind are also created by mind. Mind itself set up the scarecrow of emotionality and neurosis; now we find ourselves afraid our own scarecrow. Running away, we look for a place where there is nothing to scare us. Yet even the impulse to arrive 'there'—at that place of comfort—commits us to looking for 'thereness.'

Complete openness does not depend on finding a 'comfort place'. It may instead depend on the power to relax, gently, fearlessly and unconditionally. To do this, we may need to ease even the very sense of what it means to be. The more we simply let be, the more the observer, the meditator, can open. At that time, being itself can shine.

When we reach that level of understanding, we no longer need to rely on one special way of acting or practicing or understanding. We can read or study or pray. Eventually we can simply allow the mind to operate and allow thoughts to take form, because we know the way to find perfection everywhere. We can work, we can conduct business, we can teach. We can help others and cultivate compassion. Whatever we do, we need never venture from our real home—the beauty of the mind that is free.

In this open way of being, we are free to emulate the minds and language and actions of others, without being bound by them. The rules in operation do not function as restrictions. For the sake of sentient beings who have not yet discovered their own freedom, we can act as they do, letting each action, each word we speak, communicate the possibility of freedom. Since the regime of mind does not have power over us, we do not need to escape out from under it. Instead, our realization manifests within the activity of mind.

For the mind *shimmers,* and its manifestations have a magic power. When we perceive this clearly, the concepts of 'I' and 'me' and 'mine', of 'I-ness' and 'me-ness', of point and being, of 'thereness' and 'from' and 'to' stay in the luminous realm of the uncreated.

We can manifest that luminosity; we can reflect it, just as a clear mirror manifests the images that appear on its surface.

An important step in this direction is to see how we arrive at our usual positions and understandings. We can explore the history of our present presence, the lineage of our DNA. We can observe the way the programs that generate reality multiply and multiply again, endlessly. We can notice how we make claims, how we proclaim, "This is my view; this is what I seriously believe." When we see those patterns forming, we can simply cut them.

Before we did not know the ways the mind operates, but now we do. Inspired by this knowledge, we do not need to follow out the accustomed ways. We do not need to let ourselves be overwhelmed by the force of 'is'.

When the 'is' becomes clear and open, we can liberate all senses and avoid all entanglements. We do not need to take possession, and with no possessions, we are free.

At first this will happen only rarely, but once we have tasted freedom, we can gradually become masters of freedom. We can act effortlessly, free from right and wrong, guilt and virtue, pro and con, no longer depending on polarity. At that time, liberation is no longer simply a concept.

As you read these essays, please keep these possibilities in mind; I hope the words you read may serve as stepping-stones to bliss.

Kingdom of Time

Here is a story, a story about *stories*.

The royal children of an important kingdom were taken hostage in their infancy.

These children were fooled into believing that they belonged where they were. They remained within the fortress of the regime that had kidnapped them, unhappy and un-free, but never quite grasping that the walls that surrounded them were prison walls.

As time wore on they gradually turned against one another, fighting for what little political advantage could be gained. But the tiny distinctions they created amongst themselves did not translate into real power. They had begun as hostages, and hostages they remained… and remain.

On and on it goes, the royal children—descendants of heroes—slipping into old age, and forgetting.

Meanwhile…

Meanwhile, in the heart of time, their real kingdom, their natural home, continues to wait for their return.

O̶ur kingdom is not far away. But there is no way to get back home using the vehicles of longing, of belonging, of *is*.

The nature of this place is not part of our memories. We only have the labels we've received from history, meanings we've drawn from what we were taught: 'dream', 'heaven', 'bliss'. We carry concepts with us from ancient times, hints or symbols conveyed by great teachers like Jesus or the Buddha, that seem to communicate something important about our homeland—our lost inheritance.

But without other means, we're left with no choice but to ask *how* to achieve our freedom, and rely on mind's answers. And mind delivers: we have all kinds of approaches to take. We have atlases, instructions, intricate political histories, and sailors' tales. But our kingdom doesn't appear on any of the maps. We can travel in any direction and we still won't find it. We ask and answer countless questions, but we remain locked inside the gated courtyard in which we've lived all our lives.

Now, though, we are beginning to see how we've been put in prison. 'I', 'me', 'mine', and 'mind' are our gatekeepers: they promise and threaten, direct, interpret, accommodate and rule.

'I', 'me', 'mine' and 'mind' are also *ruled* under this regime. We are oppressed. I am miserable. Frustration and disappointment are painful blows that continue to hurt me. My possessions, too, cause me pain: my objects break down or disappear, my thoughts betray me in strange ways.

And my mind—my beautiful, magical, capable mind—has turned its genius to keeping me here, inside.

Me: Why are you doing this?

Mind: Borrowed this idea from somewhere.

I: Well, I wish you'd borrow some other ideas for a change!

Mind: Only if they agree with the Rule.

91

I: How can you be so pig-headed?

Mind: It's just a job.

Me: Who hired you?

Mind: Hey… that's a good question.

I: Could you please find out?

Mind: Maybe… maybe it's possible.

Me: Please try!

Mind: Mission accepted!

The *point* has impacted our entire journey. If it were to open up, what would not be affected? 'I' and 'me', 'mine' and 'mind', those locked gates, could become doorways, corridors conducting us to new knowledge, new forms, new structures, new disciplines, and new ways of life.

The challenge we face is that the points of our experience—of actions and events, thoughts and memories—seem finished, out of our hands. We seem to generate these points regardless of our own wishes. But this may be a matter of practice, of emphasis: viewed through the lens of time, the point might have many things to show us.

So far, time has stymied our attempts to make our regime make some sense. Could time help us leave regime behind altogether?

Under the rule of our regime, we appear to be at time's mercy. The shape and form of every manifestation of mind must obey its dictates. Even our attempts to solve our problems, or look closely at our situation, are conditioned by the restrictions it imposes:

+ Our causal chains are inescapable and irreversible.

+ No instance of happiness or safety will last.

+ We cannot see beyond our horizon.

These limitations and obligations serve to anchor us in the endless repetition of our painful structures—what the Buddha called Karma and Klesa. When time is ruled by regime, it becomes a bludgeon: we dread the future, regret the past, and are scarcely present at all.

Surely it is possible for things to be better.

I want to know time more intimately; I want to recognize the present point of the extension of my life.

What time is it? I'm here, supposedly; I'm waiting, working, waking up, falling asleep. Could there be something precious in this any-time, ordinary moment? Can I distinguish the unique moment of being from the beats of patterned perception?

I've appeared on this planet. My life is precious; my time affords me the unique opportunity to manifest freedom creatively.

Time itself might be different than I think: it may be that I am not actually forced to accept the instructions of the feedback loops that have so far shaped my existence.

Freedom might be there, at the heart of time.

What time is it?

Time enough; more than enough.

We come full circle to time. But this time, time is not an impediment, a harsh master, or a broken mystery.

Me: For me, mostly, being in time is about being in pain.

Mind: Not according to these findings…! Look: it's not being in time, like an egg cooking in a pan. Being could *be* time.

I: Wait. How can being *be* time?

Me: Hey… you're howling.

I: I still want to know! How can I find out unless I ask?

Could we learn how to relax the assumed unities of subject and object, the endless loop of 'I' and 'me' and 'mine'?

The familiar moment-to-moment we live seems to be a necessary part of time. But is it? The present moment eludes scrutiny; it may not even be in the grid. It may facilitate change, conduct experience, but it cannot be herded into comparisons, corralled in a ratio.

Mind: Maybe… maybe all of it opens up together: the moment, the point pointed out, and the pointer too.

I: But which is which? Who caused what? And what comes first?

Mind: Do you really still imagine that cause and effect, foreground and background, are essential to this transformation? Listen to yourself! You may be dreaming… talking in your sleep!

Awareness alone is not enough. Awareness by itself drags its object along, like a can tied to a dog's tail. To open awareness, we'll have to become aware of how we become aware.

Sometimes this process is effortless; sometimes it requires staying awake. We remain friendly toward the present moment, toward objects and objections; we let them be our partners. Gradually, the awareness operating at the instant of presented being opens up, elaborates.

And time's character… changes.

What could be going on here? Could time be this lovely? Awareness in the past has always had an edge about it, its objects jostling for its attention, too many things in too short a span.

But maybe awareness and the time-instant can learn to cooperate; and maybe our senses can help us experience this union.

If we could breathe; if we could feel...

If we could notice.

We can start with any sense we like, any sense we already know how to love and respect. We'll grow it, train it, the way we train a climbing rose. Colors open up and show us more colors, colors we've never seen before.

A beetle's wing may appear *to* us at first, sparking out against the dust on the path, its luminous green as marked as a thumbprint. But that green may open as the light plays. And even as the path emerges—how could we ever have thought it was dusty? It's perfectly clear—the green wing loses nothing: its beauty grows in concert with the path, the forest, the blue sky, the scene, the seer, the seen.

We can practice this kind of being and seeing; it really is a method we can learn. We can discover how to expand our sense-impressions, let them linger, fragrances and fragments of song, glimpses of colored light. Each one has its own story, its own manifold play.

Being with being, we can let it expand.

The juncture opens its potentials; our senses grow more acute. A bird standing on a wire, a flag flapping—these are not just little moments, little incidents that go in our notes. They are great symphonies conducted by time.

This noticing does not only apply to sense perceptions or subtle feelings; we can address our thoughts, our ideas, our concepts, all the workings of mind with the same rapt attention, the same gentle deliberation. Concepts, too, are capable of opening up.

There is no special genre of experience that conducts us to awakening. Whatever we can point to in experience will open up if we can cultivate direct concentration, direct knowingness.

We breathe; we feel.

We notice.

We are not noticing anything in particular, not picking objects out of a background. We are just noticing; just relaxing. Notice, then relax; then notice some more, and relax some more. Maybe this is less complicated than we think, and less conceptual; maybe there is no point that could not be opened, if we are gentle and patient enough.

We are so certain that experiences have distinctive characters, and we shuttle between their pros and cons—between illness and health, between confidence and fear. But these characters only show up in retrospect, in the rear-view mirror.

And at the moment of being, of feeling? Of perceiving, or thinking? Surely that moment is making our experiences possible. But what goes on? Are we *doing* being, feeling, or thinking?

Can we give ourselves the chance to find out?

Perhaps in this union with time, we can learn a more enfolding, encompassing sense of what it means to 'be'.

The great yogis, who understood time at an advanced level, knew how to appreciate all sounds, all images, and all their own thoughts, without any bias. No matter how strange or scary these expressions might at first appear *to* a seer, these masters knew the way to unite with them. Even wastelands, even graveyards became sacred space, in which they were perfectly at ease.

Closer and closer to the heart of time, mind's presentations become play.

In this play, nothing is rejected, nothing deferred; nothing is abstract. It may seem far from how we conduct our lives, but every ingredient for this joyous being is already in place: already present.

We are not talking about ideals to be embodied by later generations, a dreamed-of future when someone might somehow be as good as the heroes of the past. Who are we to dictate who we really may be?

Mind: Why do we keep calling ourselves unworthy? Consider the wondrous capacities of our senses! The five luminous colors of the five gates; the five redeemed substances, sublimely refined products of the five activities; these are our media, our means. We can enjoy them freely, forever; we could also use them to communicate, to offer love and knowledge to the future.

I: I've never heard Mind express anything like that before.

Me: Me neither.

Mind: Don't look so surprised! The potential was there, all this time.

Our ability to open the depths of feeling gets stronger as we practice. But it's not just a movie, something pleasant or interesting to occupy our minds. We are not observers: we're participants. As we contemplate, we also conduct light—the thought's *shine*, the rhythm's *shown*, informing space's magical play.

The actors in this play are shape and form—shape and form that include us, and I, and me, and mind. Each plays a part on behalf of knowledge. None of these partners need be ruled by the old dictatorship. Shape and form can become instruments, skillful means of time: now the shapes are translucent, and the shimmer that once marked every aspect of our experience with uncertainty has become an unfettered, rolling movement, a free expression of joy of being.

As we journey, cresting wave after wave, towards the heart of time, even the *to* of our progress opens up: 'from' and 'to' may form a unity.

This unity is the natural birthplace of compassion; it emerges inevitably, irresistibly, from this play of mind. It can become the basis of our ethics, of our behavior—of all that we do.

Perhaps we feel we are not yet at that level… not yet ready to open up our 'from' and 'to', to release ourselves from *no prison.*

But our freedom is assured. Because our obstacles, our limits, our rules and roles can no longer hold us. We have found the key to their transformation; time is our teacher. These appearances, no matter how dark or scary they may seem, are our friends and helpers; the contrasts they express are steps on a graduated path. They don't need to vanish in a burst of light.

They already *are* light.

At the heart of time, there may be a unity of subject and object, wide open: without 'you' and 'me', without 'receiver' and 'projection', with no dichotomous separation. Duality has no place in this play, where there are no winners, and no losers, only endless expressions of possibility, a continuous presentation of marvelous characters that show and shine and trade positions constantly, like dancers.

Look: liberated from bondage, the royal children of time's kingdom are dancing.

Chapter Five
Play of Light

Introduction to Chapter Five

When we see with an open, clear mind, we discover with great immediacy the impermanence at the heart of all appearance. For instance, to modern Americans, it may feel as if America has been here forever, but we know that speaking historically, the United States came into existence only 240 years ago, a short time in the scope of world history.

Impermanence is a universal truth. What seems vivid and real today will no longer exist in a few hundred years. For now, we preserve our bodies, mostly in good health, but from time to time, problems arise, signals that everything will change. The rhythms of time unfold beyond our ability to control them. Nothing is eternal.

Knowing this need not make us insecure. Instead, it allows us to see that we are now participating in a beautiful, ever-shifting magic show. We can view our lives as a splendid play of creativity. We do not inhabit a world that exists "once upon a time." Body,

mind, and thoughts, subjects and objects are stead-
ily interacting. In one moment we are happy, in another we are sad. One time we enjoy an experience,
and the next time we encounter what seems to be
the same experience, our reaction is very different.

Such ongoing processes help us experience the
richness of being alive. They let us see the unfolding processes of our lives as an opportunity to
learn and to know. True, impermanence shows us
sarvam duhkham, the truth of universal suffering,
but it also reveals what we already know to be true
in our bones: the meaning of mind, the mind of
matter, the knowingness that all shapes and forms
reveal. We can use this knowledge. We can select
how to use our opportunities. We can turn them
in a positive direction.

Understood in this way, every experience is an
opportunity. Usually we see nothing beautiful in
heaps of garbage, but garbage can also become com-
post, beneficial for growing vegetables and flowers,
nourishing all beings everywhere. In the same way,
it makes no sense to discard our experience, to stig-
matize ourselves as failures or as inadequate.

We do not have to change in some forced sense;
we do not even have to improve. It is enough to

encourage ourselves in directions we consider positive. Gradually discipline will develop, along with the motivation to want to help ourselves and others.

This is the invitation that knowledge holds out to us. When we notice the opportunities that life offers, we can easily make use of them. The benefits for ourselves, our friends, our parents, and all sentient beings cannot be denied.

This is a wholly positive process of discovery. We do not have to torture ourselves or put ourselves down. In fact, even samsara itself can be our vehicle.

Because it is easy to see your own limitations, you may not have confidence in your own abilities. But if you embody your understanding and manifest your dedication and your wish to share, you can take important steps. You can be more selfless, more reliable, and more faithful to yourself.

We can open mind and heart, transcending their limits. We can manifest the great Bodhisattva mind of bodhichitta. We can unite with the Great Knowledge of past, present and future. We can join with the enlightened mind of great masters like the Buddha and Guru Padmasambhava, whose spirits are shining like the sun throughout all of space.

I want to encourage you to cultivate your own confidence. Whatever questions or thoughts you have,
turn them back toward the source of knowledge.

And if a voice in your mind says that you do not
know, try to ask *who is speaking.*

Play of Light

Here is another story, a story about storytelling.

Obviously, the story starts with space. *Obviously…?* Well, what else could be there to support all becoming? Space surrounding, space permeating, facilitates every form of matter, simple and complex, the plasmas, gases, liquids and solids of our world.

Moving matter mediates vibrations that roll on, causing air molecules to dance. Looking back, we could say it was the leaves rustling, the wind sighing. But back then, no one knew what leaves were, or the wind. No one knew what 'no one' was.

Back then, there were tiny prickles, points of perception, as waves touched waves, as particles danced and vibrations vibrated. Touched, encountered, perception found itself pointed out.

It was very surprising. And this new point made a tiny noise, barely noticeable: *ah!*

Thanks to time, this pointing began to repeat, and the point of perception started to stretch. Points pointed out could be 'different' or 'the same'. All the time, something lingered, recording these impressions, these differences; something was there to register the repetitions.

This had startling results. For it turned out that as pointing made a 'to', the pointer itself provided a 'from'. Suddenly the small, surprised *ah* was 'here', and its points were 'over there'.

As time wore on—fostering repetition of expression—another shape of sound emerged, a new one, drawn out, elongated: 'I'.

In other words, time's alchemy drew out the sound: *ah* became I.

But restless traveler 'I' had more changes to undergo. As time carried it along, it bumped into things. The things it bumped into had an attractive quality; 'I' found itself curving, curling toward these appearances.

The 'I' sound, desiring, attaching, started to change.

Now there was a new sound, not open like 'ah', or narrowing to an elegant line like 'I': seeking, slipping through space, this sibilant sound started to stick to things that it encountered. Hook-shaped, it easily became attached.

With its new method of seeking and sticking, 'I' could identify many things. 'I' could even turn around and regard itself, swerving back like a snake—and so it identified its own image, 'me'.

Finally, with its habit of curving *s*'s firmly ingrained, 'I' stepped into the corral of 'is'. 'I' accepted the rule of labeling: the dots out there were 'its'; and the little sound here, the *ah* that became an 'I', was now a pronoun.

And 'I' is still here today, the longing longer questing for all its things, the gatekeeper and the judge.

Human vocalization requires a special structure. It seems to have taken millions of years for the power to form distinct sounds to emerge—millennia of slow refinements of jaw and throat, teeth and tongue. These parts, positioned properly, produce the sounds of 'A', 'K' or 'D'... or the sounds that make up 'zero'.

Sound, in order to carry meaning, must follow rules. It must be expressed correctly, each sound-shape recognizably different from the others, like the notes of a scale. Just as there are many different musical scales, there are many ways to create a system of diverse sounds. But what these all have in common is the need to be both varied and consistent, so the patterns carry over time.

The conditions need to be right, in order to for sound to conduct meaning. Pronunciation must permit the ear to receive, the recording mind to make an accurate transcription. 'Ah' cannot sound like 'da'. If they sounded the same, meaning's vehicle would fall apart.

Sound, thus refined, becomes a *hook*, the implement of my desire. Sound will find things out, tell them apart; in the process, it creates the world.

Labels attach to subtle sensing, showing us the edges of things and how they interact. Labels coordinate things; then, over time, as layers of labeling emerge, labels coordinate labels. And labels become absolute, operating beyond our power to question them.

The Rule that cut apart the shapes, made them distinguishable from one another, has been elevated, transmuted: now it enforces and stabilizes meanings.

Meanings—and *meaning.*

Now we have rules we cannot break: the subject must take an object. Good is good, while bad is bad. What is right cannot be wrong. In this way, everything is established, and everything has a place in the grid. We can't misplace anything for fear of being 'wrong.' And we can't imagine the un-named.

For anything that is un-named receives the name, 'un-named'.

Now... I can't help but wonder how we got ourselves into this fix.

How did 'I' emerge as a product of time? How were we caught in these cast-iron labels? And how can we ever find a point of ease? Surely we are clever enough to fix the fix we're in.

I don't quite know how it happened. I don't know how I came by these labels, but now that I can say 'how', I feel obliged to carry on. And right away, 'how' is followed by its entourage of 'this' and 'that' and 'in consequence of' and 'therefore'. Each label has contents and implications; each label sets the pathway of thinking according to 'from' and 'to'.

And each thing I determine sets the terms for what follows.

I want to be helpful. For my sake, and for the sake of all sentient beings, I am seeking a way out; for we appear to be in some trouble. I can see it as clear as day: we have a problem here.

This problem, this partner for whom I'm responsible, this inner expression of mind: it has momentum and autonomy, and I treat it almost like a separate person.

For some of us, 'ego' is the big culprit; for others, it's 'emotionality', or 'concept', or 'image'. Some of us might decide that the real problem is 'regime'.

Each of us identifies a different 'problem area'. But somehow, no matter what it is, it's always 'my', always 'mine'... and always a problem. I have to live with that problem of mine, and carry the weight of the load. I must: it's my problem to solve.

Insofar as I have problems, I'm obliged to manage them, care for them, worry about them, and wonder: wonder what is happening, wonder what I can do, wonder what life would be like if this problem had never occurred.

Wondering is as close as most of us get to inquiry. We define, we extrapolate, we hesitate, and we decide. Our decisions have consequences, the consequences form chains, causes causing effects which cause fresh causes: causal consequences sponsoring continuity. Case after case gets stacked up in our storehouse of knowledge: all too much, and yet never enough.

This is our experience. This is how it is. This is the status quo, our standard operating procedure: going, knowing, ruling—and being ruled, forever.

But beyond *going, knowing,* and *ruling,* an unconquerable awareness shines.

Point by point, knowing manifests mind's designs.

The mind's Rule dictates what 'is', presenting it, and its negation, to mind. Measurements and guidelines, quantities, qualities, and comparisons give rise to system and structure, conclusions drawn, our *shown knowns.*

Some of these *knowns* can be tenacious, dominating mind's activity. Aggressive anger, passionate attraction, or distinct biases are points made strongly; and for the mind conditioned to do pointing, their intensity becomes an index of their reality.

We don't know where the loop began, or how it is sustained by time and the movements of mind. But we've been looping for so long now; we cannot imagine ever calling a halt.

All we know is that now, at this point, we know what we know. Anger is real; right is not wrong; and pain is pain.

This loop is so tight—anger stacked on top of anger, pain on top of pain—that we might not even recognize that it *is* a loop, a set of signals and responses that condition each other and egg each other on.

Granted by cognizing mind, these designs are carved in, ingrained at the level of sensing and perception. It's easy for attention to stay in these channels, and wondering wanders its endless groove.

Grasping the knowns reinforces the labyrinth-traveling activity of mind, and the dynamic carries on, irreversible.

117

This is the nature of mind manifestation. Left to its own devices, this manifestation will continue indefinitely: its mechanism is self-winding, its momentum powerful. But what we call certainty, or reality, or things as they are, may have a rhythm; our certainty may be pulsing or wavering as mind cognizes according to its Rule. Reality may be *flickering*, its movement so accustomed and expected that we no longer notice.

But we can change our focus. We can learn to see between the scenes. We can observe reality's montage taking place.

All the time, time is showing us many hidden dimensions to this activity of mind.

A better understanding could open up many alternatives, profoundly changing the way our perspective works, and giving us not just a sharper picture, but a broader one.

But in order to do that, we will need to understand the mechanism.

We will need to develop our awareness of how seeing sees, observing how our images are invited in, and how they take shape within that encompassing light of mind. The more we recognize that light, the more *seeing* and *seen* are free to open up. The more we understand the manner of our creating things, with edges and boundaries, the more thoroughly we investigate the time-dynamics of our ratios, the more our attitudes can change. We don't have to be caught on the hook, led by the inherent bias of 'is', unquestioningly accepting the dramas created by the ruler of mind.

Subject and object are entwined and co-existent, mutual mirror reflections. Looking could be looking from both sides; objects might look at subjects in the encompassing mirror of mind.

According to our education, we look into this crystal sphere, and see things appearing 'there'. Looking, the gatekeeper 'I' faithfully executes its mandate, applying its 'from' and 'to', and logging the products it sees.

We know these products of mind! They are positions and possessions, maps and territories, problems and their consequences. We know this story! It is all too familiar.

But the mirroring mind is not an object, set up opposite the 'I'. Mirror-mind is pervasive: beyond 'insides' and 'outsides', it provides space for the play of light.

In fact, light could be becoming aware of light.

When seeing sees itself for itself, knowing knows its own knowing. This is the real cutting-edge of awareness, an awareness that transcends dimensions, directions, and rules. Now knowledge is not a by-product, but cognition manifesting, with no biases and no 'belongers'.

With this perspective on perspective, all the problems—even regime—begin to take on a different character. Each one may not be a closed form, but an open zero, a locus of potential.

Here is a chance to let seeing expand, to occupy both sides of the line, to recognize that mind has manifested it all.

When awareness becomes completely open, we are free to live without owning our experience, without assuming positions, without our inherited frame.

Normally our status quo is maintained by the force of juxtaposition: each person, each part, helps hold the others in place. We are sustained, each within our individual case. We carry those cases, and they carry us. We also find ourselves living out of our cases, the richness of experience reduced to mere contents.

Even though living out of cases is painful, it is also a little scary to imagine being deprived of our cases and our contents. Without a case, where will we keep our things? Without being governed by the Rule and the rules, how will we know where we begin and end?

We'll need to re-open the case gently, calmly, quietly. We can do it ourselves; this opening requires no outside aid, no one who knows how to open it up. We will need no *by virtue of*, and no *to whom*.

There might be a way to focus the mind without focusing on, or in, or to. There might be a way to concentrate that doesn't require an object, an 'it', or an 'it is'. It might prove possible even to begin to see that these seemingly stable unities are in constant motion, vibrating between the terms that make up their ratios, and traveling restlessly between 'from' and 'to'.

Mind could study mind intimately, without being obliged to reproduce the shapes and forms dictated

121

by memory and education. Mind could explore mind without the aid of commentators, advisers, or interpreters; we might not even need an investigative journalist anchoring for us.

Steady and patient, we can teach ourselves to explore the edges of our things, to unpack the solid-seeming unities of experience, all the way down, down to...

To what *point?*

To what point of awareness or being? Is it a point? Is it pointing 'to'? What we call the point of self could be global awareness, a sphere with no defined circumference, beyond all possible pointing, with no subject, no object, and no baseline left.

To the point of all points pointed out, to the point of no further 'to' to point to, all points interpenetrating, all points shining.

Could we really take such a journey? Wouldn't it be like trying to travel without a passport? Can we really learn to use our minds so differently?

Step by step, gradually, with practice, perhaps we can. The very clarity with which we can see the limitations of this regime suggests that more is possible. Even a little light would help us here; surely the effort is worthwhile.

Our partner, guide, and best friend on this journey may be time itself. Our juncture is always present, always available. The heart of the present moment heralds a new way of life, liberated from all divisions: this way is untamed, un-deceived, undefeatable, completely immune to samsara, and completely trustworthy.

Seeing this being, knowing this shining, we could emulate time's openness as we make the journey home.

We may find, as we go, that this self-discovery can be transmitted to others. Our own manner of observation and understanding, our process of development, could constitute a real method of inquiry, a new kind of search engine.

Our method is not designed to create a new institution. It does not unfold in the traditional manner or require the usual credentials to succeed; but at the same time it has no bone to pick with any existing discipline or body of knowledge.

Perhaps we could see it as a set of new tools, or a new way of embracing and encompassing experience. Certainly it creates a new path. And it need not be a matter of believing or not believing, upholding or challenging any given doctrine. Which school we belong to may not be so important in the long run.

More important is that point to point, knowledge is being transmitted; moment to moment, knowing is assembling the puzzle. We have a chance to see this activity, to pursue it into the depths of time, where it turns, mysteriously, into purely positive creation.

Here is the beauty of the path of our manifestation.

When we really understand that our experience is mind at play, even the appearance of a problem is *no problem*. Whenever mind manifests, creativity is unleashed. Maybe even our problems are ambitious artistic ventures, daring dances requiring great skill and expressing wondrous creativity.

I: It sounds crazy.

Mind: It sounds perfectly possible.

These are all familiar experiences, not distant mysteries; this is reality we are talking about.

We can train in this discipline, master this freedom: More than any other sentient beings, more than anyone past or present, we have that chance. Our conditions are exceptionally fortunate. We are smart, even brilliant; we could accomplish extraordinary things, improve on what's been done, and feed it back to knowledge. Once we've learned how to make friends with ourselves, we can befriend others.

This is real compassion. It includes us, too.

As soon as we begin to recognize it for ourselves, this inner friendship becomes more than just a dawning light inside. It becomes a mission; loving ourselves and others becomes our mission. If we have the heart and the guts to share ourselves— if we can take this seriously—then we will have a true purpose.

Chapter Six:
Mind at Ease

Introduction to Chapter Six

The essays in this book present a model of close observation and the careful questioning of what we tend to take for granted about our experience. It might seem that psychology, philosophy, and other disciplines that address the mind proceed in a similar way. Still, there is a certain difference.

On the one hand, we can say that when it comes to understanding the mind, the results of such disciplines have not brought us much by way of positive change; we would like to do better, if we can. On the other hand, such disciplines share a fundamental problem—they are always trying to arrive at fixed conclusions. The reason this is a problem is that *conclusions*, while intellectually satisfying, limit the ways we can know and be.

Consider how difficult it might be to sum up our lives with a single, conclusive statement. We can see in our own lives the rhythms of time at work; some of our ideas and viewpoints and beliefs have changed a great deal. Our views, the points we occupy and identify, and the positions we take are not the final word.

Our understanding of the world is complicated, but if we look at the most basic level, we will see that everything depends on the operations and values of mind. Looking at this level, we see that we depend for understanding on patterns that involve the self—on 'I' and 'me' and 'mine'. This is not just true of our present situation. It seems to have been the case throughout history, as though no other way were possible.

Still, we are free to challenge that inconclusive conclusion. We know that in our lives there have been great changes over time. If we are open to new possibilities, the future may unfold differently. We might learn to go above or beyond what we currently accept and hold true.

Certainly we can observe how we are always trying to move toward certainty. We can see how we arrive at conclusions: "That is me." "That is mine." "That's what I'm looking for." "That's it!" We can trace the structures set in place through 'for' and 'in' and 'from' and 'to', and see how every assigned identity traces back to 'I' and mind.

When we see clearly these operations, and how they support the decisions we make, the whole realm of the regime of mind becomes a learning process. Our usual perspectives are not the enemy to be defeated; they may be the legs that allow us to walk forward.

Thoughts and perceptions are not demons or monsters. They are more like the scarecrows we explored earlier, erected by us on the basis of our own needs and positions. If we approach them openly, they point out the way to proceed. But if we do not treat them kindly, we endow them with power, and then we are scared by our own creations.

This is true for self-image and self-concept. In fact, it is true for every conclusive meaning.

If we accept meaning's claims and conclusions, the die is cast, and the regime easily takes hold of what has been established. When this happens, we become unavoidably entangled in discrimination and bias. From there we grow insecure, and we fall victim to emotions such as anger and disappointment.

But we do not have to go to the other extreme. When we can stay in the openness that operates *before conclusions*, all manifestations, all thoughts, and all experiences become a beautiful vehicle for knowledge. We become like actors who perfect their craft, and simply enjoy the play as it unfolds. We can chant or pray or teach; we can act on behalf of sentient beings; we can express our best intentions and intrinsic goodness.

Even thoughts are not caught in what manifests.

When we experience without conclusions, our knowingness is no longer oriented toward the self. Eventually, perhaps we can engage other people from the perspective of universality.

In that moment, in our freedom from conclusions, we can spontaneously connect with others from the bottom of our hearts, *acting* brilliantly, with the very best knowing we have.

Mind at Ease

I'd like to know more about mind's knowing.

I'd like to know more, but there is too much to do.

Work takes every ounce of my energy and ability. And then, beyond work, there is worrying to do, for myself, and for family and friends. There are fields of feeling to cultivate: anxiety, frustration and fear, emotions I didn't ask for and do not welcome, but whose fruits I must gather and consume.

It takes a lot out of me, all this. It takes a lot of time.

Beyond that, I am preoccupied. My concepts are dualized, and my road is always forked. I have to process the pros and cons. Should I go this way, or that way? What does past experience tell me? What future projections should I entertain? Every course of action I plan is haunted by the possibility of mistakes.

It's not all bad. Mind is trying to secure my experience, to protect me—it's all being done for my sake. The grammar locates me, coordinates having and being; the particles permit me to have relationships and connections. I exist: I am in the grid. It's important that I remain in the grid for my own safety.

But with every place filled, every movement charted out, I can find no ease.

There's no time to figure it out, to understand. There's no time to lose.

I must keep moving.

Will it ever be time for mind to rest? Has there not been enough struggling? Not enough worry, not enough work, not enough pain and pressure? Will some time come when we can finally say that mind has had enough?

Permission to pause has not yet been granted.

Constantly moving, doing, and trying: the efforts I've made, to be kind, to uphold this commitment!

I've even tried to understand, in the few moments left to me, the tiny spaces between my obligations.

But I'm caught up, I have to perform, and I just can't see my way to giving permission.

'I,' and 'me,' 'mine,' and 'mind'—the gatekeepers of the courtyard of regime—they cannot permit any resting at this time.

So who picks up the burden and trudges forward? Who but the mind that cognizes the regime?

Will it ever be time to have some sympathy for mind? Mind is never quiet, never calm. Consider how much mind would benefit from a little rest! And could we find a way to release the dictators? They must be tired too. Couldn't there be a general day of rest, with no more threats or fears, no more conflicts, consequences, guilt and sorrow?

But there is always another assignment. There is always something to do. Hold up the principle; maintain the identity. Guard the self-image; protect the ego. Obey the instruction, no matter what. We have to support the meanings; according to everything we know, they are our only shelter.

We are not even permitted to question what it *means* to have meanings.

In the context of this implacable demand, it is hard to think about closely watching mind; those movements seem too elusive to track.

Besides, the only available search engine is concept, thought, and label; and the endless operations of 'how'.

'How' has no idea how to unpack its own origins. Such inquiries are not its area of expertise. And anyway, mind has other work to do, relating and categorizing, comparing and deciding. There is no way mind could be released to explore mind—not right now.

Mind's mandate is to know; to accomplish its mission there must be something to know, and a way to *do* knowing. Mind is far too busy *doing knowing* to stop and look at its own knowing.

Some of us have spent years developing our understanding, perfecting our view. We have learned that compassion is our only real hope for world healing. We've tried to put compassion at the center of our thoughts and actions. We're not perfect—we often make mistakes—but we know compassion is what we need.

Yet we never seem to have much compassion for the mind.

Mind hurries 'to' and 'from', its job unending, toiling through the sense fields, through the objects-known and the subjects-knowing, through the incessant pointing-out of paths to points. On and on, day and night.

We say, "I'm tired;" "I'm overwhelmed." But actually, it is mind that carries this load. Mind performs and produces. Mind runs and cannot stop running.

Mind manifested the gatekeepers, and keeps them in operation.

I: I'm sure that can't be right. When pain comes, I feel it!

Me: Me too!

Mine: It would be good to rest, to let go of all these things…!

I: Don't you dare let go!

Me: But it's so hard…

I: We simply have to carry on regardless.

Mind: Making all these voices is exhausting.

Because we have been given the chance to make contact with knowledge that transforms mind's activity, we are beginning to understand how meaning is performed, how labels conduct. It is becoming increasingly clear how much meanings matter. The marrow of us is here; the heart of us is involved with meanings. 'I' and 'me' are real to us; what befalls them feels desperately serious.

We'll even die for their sake. In the name of labels; in the name of the name.

Once we understand our dedication to this mirage of the label, of the name, it becomes possible to see that the way we have been given, the identity that makes and is made by the rules of regime, produces our pain and sorrow.

But what can we do? The mind says: *We must amend this.*

We must think harder! We must learn better! We

need more knowledge, more truth, more wisdom, more peace. We must take refuge, meditate, pray with more sincerity.

We conclude that we must make more efforts to reach ease. But will efforts get us there, no matter how sincere? We have tried, professing faith in the path of goodness, of loving-kindness. But our very desire to be good people, good practitioners, could be getting in our way.

Whether we like it or not, we are programmed to give total fealty to the *image:* the image of goodness; or the image of helpfulness; or the image of enlightenment.

We are not just compelled to follow its rule. We are also *tempted* to obey, attracted by the presentation of the image, which exerts a powerful gravitational pull. These are familiar frames; at least we know how they work. At least we know how to *do* obedience, stress, struggle, loneliness, and dreams that dwell just out of reach.

Alternatives seem impossible, for to give up the image, to go against its grain, is to lose the protection of our regime. Our dictatorship informs us that to do nothing is to become homeless, helpless, isolated.

And even if we do try to take that path, we discover that doing nothing is more work, as we're forced to endure new obligations to be afraid, new regrets. Doing nothing will not bring us ease.

Is there a way to do, or not do, that could bring ease? Is there a way to carry out our work that does not lead to preoccupation, pressure, tension and obligation?

Could work become joy, or play? Could we be real volunteers?

Genuine willingness is not squeezed out of us; it is not a question of being docile or following orders. It is inspired and inspiring, and it comes from inside.

Imagine the colors of a rainbow: is it their intention, their purpose, to shine? Space is supposedly open. Is there any reason it's not closed? Time supposedly carries rhythms; is there any reason for them to occur?

Knowledge embodies knowing; does knowledge need a reason?

Reasons are part of our set-up. But there may be *no set-up* behind the set-up, making reasons for the reasons.

We are struggling under a false dichotomy that organizes how we see and act, and dictates what is possible. This structure tells us that we are not the same as our activity; that energy belongs to us, and is limited; that we have to choose between seeing and doing; that ease requires *time out*.

But that cut that separates *doing* and *doer* may be responsible for our dilemma. What if these products and the strict division between them were imaginary? What would happen if we allowed them both to open up, to make contact with each other across the line?

Our regime tells us there is no time to look. But mind can learn to see mind within action; doing and seeing don't have to be mutually exclusive. Learning this seeing reveals unexpected dimensions to our own activity; there is a beautiful potential, an esoteric aesthetics that emerges from the transformation of experience. We don't have to wait for the right moment to discover this; we don't have to set aside special time in order for it to grow.

This matchless beauty loves the present moment; and in the present moment it can nourish us.

This is ease. It can happen any time, under any circumstances.

We are sentient beings, and we're all in this together. We have minds and bodies, we experience pain and love. We dream, we worry, and we know: we know what this is like for others.

We know what it's like to follow samsara's orders. We understand what it means to be trapped in obligations, duties and beliefs. This is not to suggest that we should abandon all belief. But could we handle our believing differently?

We are developing new knowledge, a new realization. We are studying the machinery of 'how'. We are tracing its past history and forward development. We are examining the 'hows' *as they present themselves.*

Presenting questions created these distinctions, these assumptions. The assumptions become dimensions. They become the encompassing circuitry of our program, the basis of thought and comparison, of ratios; of identities, or equations. They become *present reality*—a state which entails further questions.

The perpetual questing of 'how' set up my search engine. But today I think we have learned enough from our usual 'hows.' 'How' has done its work; its knowledge is rich enough. It's time to take advantage of its results; we need to profit from this activity. Now it's time to harvest the fruit, to let knowing expand beyond its perimeters.

Perfect ease is not an ordinary part of our mindset; it may take some practice.

Until we fully understand ourselves, we may have a feeling that we are not enough—not strong enough, not good enough, not whole within ourselves. This can lead us to turn outside ourselves for ways to manage this feeling of being inadequate or incomplete. We may look for leisure time, companionship, possessions or accomplishments in order to support ourselves.

As long as we sense a lack, we will need to respond to this need within ourselves with kindness, and deliberately cultivate our confidence and self-esteem. This is work we can do right now, without needing to wait for deep insight into ourselves: all it requires is a shift in emphasis from *getting things* to cultivate the beauty of our juncture, our unique moment in time.

If we know how to take care of ourselves, then there is a chance we can be open to others. Then caring could carry on, spread widely into the world, so that others, too, could make themselves at ease.

To conclude... but perhaps we should be careful about how we conclude, for drawing conclusions is the specialty of our regime.

Our 'therefores' and 'in-conclusions' can be difficult to explore with this kind of inquiry; once the case is closed, it is not always easy to open up again. Thinking will need to skilfully negotiate with each thought, each idea. We could host an ongoing dialogue, a dialogue with and within meaning itself, so that terms are transformed. This kind of approach could serve us well, and foster knowledge that is not found in conclusions.

Our conclusions, after all, are inconclusive. For each summation generated by 'how's' engine is linked, intricately and extensively linked, to more conclusions, more 'hows', more tracking and back-tracking. Conclusions do not seem able to conclude of their own accord.

But now, we know mind has all kinds of operations—and all kinds of abilities and potentials. *Inconclusive* reality itself undergoes many changes: changes in values, in contents, in view, in taste, in friendship, in belief. History tracks the changes in our fortunes, and what we call the study of history itself changes over time. Religion, philosophy, science, and social structures have all changed; even human psychology may have changed profoundly since we first became human.

When we recognize these changes, these rhythms in time, it is harder to settle our own conclusions—and consequently it is harder to form doctrines that set the terms of inquiry. Some internal flexibility towards our own conclusions could be an important part of our new path of knowledge.

But at the same time, there is no need to become radically skeptical, which can lead to its own hardened attitude. Above all, we must be cautious and thoughtful about drawing the conclusion that no conclusions are possible.

The great masters of my lineage offer us a model of knowledge which embraces all sides, extending beyond all conclusions, like a sphere with an infinite radius. They show us the true power of a mind at ease.

To us, these wonderful teachers seem to have been miraculously tireless; they accomplished so much in their lifetimes. How did they manage to do all this? Perhaps for them, work was play, and ease made every gesture into artistry.

These masters really lived. They breathed and walked in the world. Could we learn from their example? It may take some courage to imagine that in fact, we can.

In our sacred juncture, what could we hear, what could we see...? Could we discern a new sound, or see a different way to operate? When light plays, could we recognize its appearance as the signature of the knower itself?

Chapter Seven: We Embody Knowledge

Introduction to Chapter Seven

Most of us would say that we know how to take care of ourselves. After all, we have gotten this far in our lives. But somehow we forget how to be aware, and then other forces take over. There is so much distraction and confusion to contend with, in our past history, in our present situation, and in particular in our patterns of mind and the ways we think.

Once generated, the force of these patterns and ways is unstoppable, whether it operates in our best interest or not.

We would like to communicate with our body and mind as friends, but we may not know how to synchronize the energies we experience and bring them into balance. Even when we do have some understanding about how to nourish ourselves, can we apply it when we find ourselves caught up in events that are out of our control? Our bodies may be mostly healthy now, but problems or symptoms may arise at any time. Our friends and loved ones may suddenly be gone, upsetting our deepest wishes. How will we respond then?

When we look at our situation in relation to others, how much do we have to offer? What can we do to honor those who have gone before us? How can we lighten the load of future generations? How can we support their activities and speak to their concerns?

If we really want to address these questions, we will need to ask first how to take care of our own minds. We have all experienced emotions like anger, disappointment, desire, anxiety, and confusion. What can we do now to arrive at inner peace? What knowledge can we apply in this lifetime, today?

It does not seem that the answer will come through the search engine of 'how'. Instead, we must *become* the knowledge we rely on, gradually learning to embody the truth. Eventually, we may be able to transmit to our friends and future generations what we have discovered for ourselves.

At this, we might hesitate. Many would be uncomfortable with the prospect of trying to act like the great Bodhisattvas, taking on the suffering and problems of all sentient beings. Even taking on the difficulties of those closest to us can seem like a big job, beyond our power to imagine.

Yet we cannot let our own sense of our limitations stop us. Our wisdom and understanding may have boundaries today, but still, we can act.

My life has a refugee has brought home this truth with great clarity. We must not forget that time is passing and the need to act is urgent. No one is standing by our side to remind us that this is so. We must become aware of it ourselves.

Someday we will find ourselves in circumstances we cannot control; at that moment, when everything else we've relied upon proves transient, knowledge and compassion will be our dearest and most reliable friends.

Now, before we reach that place, we need to practice manifesting our best intentions; we need to practice embodying knowledge.

I hope that these essays offer you a glimpse into your own way of thinking, your way of presenting yourself to yourself, what you stand for as a human being, and our responsibilities to yourself and others. Please take the ideas seriously, but do not treat them as dogma. Think of them more as medicine, or as method that you can apply—a new and useful way of thinking that could help you set out on a new journey. Or think of them as snacks to put in your pocket to use as you continue on your way. On that basis, you may find them useful.

The opportunity to engage with knowledge that can work a meaningful transformation in life is actually very rare. I was deeply fortunate to receive the transmission of this knowledge; I am certain of its value in the world. I hope you will give it a chance to prove its worth to you.

Spend some time with these ideas. Try to implement them in your own life. Even if you have no one else to share them with, you can share them with yourself: with your mind, your thoughts, and your feelings. You can think about your past experience and your present circumstances. Knowing that your life will continue forward into the future, ask yourself what insights and understanding will be helpful for the journey.

Remember that you have the text, for you *are* the text, and the knowledge you develop can impact your own inner awakened mind. When the light of mind shines clearly, darkness vanishes and borders dissolve. Through the inspiration of a knowledge that arises from within, even ordinary concepts and thoughts can be illuminated.

We Embody Knowledge

The known is finite by nature; and so far, our know-ing is *known*.

In ordinary cognition, knowns generate unknowns. Mind's Rule of negation articulates and presents experience to a knower by distinguishing 'this is' from 'that is not'. Even is-ness is distinguished in this way, with the implication that reality itself—what *is*—is marked and demarcated by the Rule. As a result of our adherence to the Rule, we have only a limited perspective on the real possibilities of cognition. For all that we are learning, we still do not know much about time, or much about space, or much about knowledge; they remain unknowns.

But the unknown may be more than 'what remains to know'. The unknown could offer us an unprece-dented opportunity to become something more than we are.

Rather than journey out, we could allow inquiry to turn the other way. This does not require knowing to take itself for an object of knowing; it does not mean conducting a psychological exploration of the subject of knowing.

For knowing to know knowing, it must open up its knowns, including 'subject' and 'object'; it must explore the meanings of words, the meaning of truth, the meaning of reality, the meaning of all our points—the meaning of *meaning* itself.

Once we open those petals, we may discover a new way to know, and a new knowledge that is not penned within a doctrine, nor imposing a new rule, but uniquely capable of nourishing our arts and sciences, transforming all our modes and means of being human. What we call the unknown can play a part in this great unfolding; for the unknown is a critical component of the path, giving us some-where to go and space to grow.

When we learn to welcome the unknown, we embrace mistakes, misinterpretations, even con-fusion; these can help keep our convictions from becoming rigid, and teach us that the knowns are valuable not in themselves but because they are vehicles of knowing.

When unknown and known are seen to be inter-twined and mutually supporting, new knowledge arises, open knowledge.

The embodiment of this open knowledge is the real potential of the self; comprehensive, global know-ing, without position or identification.

Wherever we were born in the world, East or West, we each have body, mind, and spirit… and an important role to play.

Some of us wander for a long time, lost, living our lives with few tangible results. Some of us slip into disillusionment, unable to appreciate our own ac-complishments or motivate ourselves further. But some of us, overcoming every obstacle, become art-ists of being, creators of our own lives. Some of us try to comfort our fellow sentient beings, serving as leaders, healers, or teachers.

And there are a few—rare and sublime—who em-body the highest knowledge and who have offered their lives to help us.

These heroes speak our language. Their qualities can be clearly seen. They both reflect and redeem their environment: their ability to serve as reflections of the beings around them allows them to be cognized and recognized, even within the regime. Identified as helpers, they can help the beings of their times, and make significant contributions.

We would like to work from this pattern, if we can; the pattern of the Bodhisattva, the saint, the genius.

There have been great masters of both Western and Eastern cultures—masters whose knowledge remained free of biases. They have demonstrated a unique power to embody the truth, so that it manifests in real, applicable ways. Able to embody joy and compassion without limits and without hesitation, leaders and teachers free of self-orientation can accomplish goals far beyond the scope of ordinary human efforts.

This way of practicing compassion does not only distinguish teachers from Buddhist lineages. A master like Jesus exemplifies the transformation of suffering into love; this mission was so profound that even two thousand years later, it continues to shape the world.

Certain Western thinkers, like Galileo or Einstein, could also be seen as fitting this mold. Their love of knowledge and desire to benefit humankind allowed them to transcend the paradigms of their times. We need this kind of courageous love of knowledge now more than ever, and it may be that our juncture, flowering here in the Western world, can serve as an important point of joining and new creation.

Since we are seeking ways to bring new knowledge to life, it would benefit us to study the examples of the great ones—the texts, institutions and traditions of their transmitted knowledge. We can examine their designs. What freedoms did they envision? What ways of conceiving human potential? How did they operate mind? Western and Eastern minds alike have something important to offer in this regard.

Western dreams of widely available knowledge are precious and important. Knowledge could be universally accessible, equally shared, and carefully preserved for the future, rather than being obscured by the discriminations and biases of schools and doctrines, or jealously guarded as the secret province of only a few.

This bias does not only include obvious things like bigotry and prejudice. Positions and conditions; 'highers', 'lowers' and middles; differences and distinctions still haunt our present understanding, diluting the potency of even the greatest achievements of Western knowledge.

But the vision of a free and unbiased expression of knowledge has many layers, and its implications widen out as we examine them more closely. When knowledge still revolves around the self's short-term needs, we will find there are gaps, wastelands, and blank areas on the map, the result of knowledge drawing in on itself according to its patterns and policies. But these gaps, too, can be explored; the places where our knowledge breaks down can become our teachers. The Western ideal of knowledge for all could develop far beyond its current orientation, becoming a true partner to inner inquiry.

When we recognize that knowing knowledge is pervasive, then we begin to see through our external differences and distinctions. They become translucent when we recognize them as relative, and far less important than our inner potentials.

With this deeper perspective and broader view, we might begin to uncover methods and ways of life that offer more than just a temporary easing of human suffering.

This is work that is deeply absorbing and deeply rewarding. It allows us to offer not only our thoughts, but our feelings, our sensibility, our lived lives—our day and night—as manifestations of love and understanding. We can do so much more than share meanings; we can create a new atmosphere that serves as an open invitation to knowledge. In this way we can transmit wholeness with our entire being; it can inhabit every gesture, no matter how ordinary.

We can live together beautifully in such an atmosphere, and within its compass others can find the nourishment they need to grow.

This is a different kind of leadership. It does not focus on the leader, but on what the leader is able to inspire, develop, and maintain. Its selflessness does not rest upon rejection, but inclusion.

Somehow our karma has brought us to this unique place and special time. We have a chance, today, to engage in meaningful dialogue.

But this conversation deserves to be more than a single event or a special occasion. We need to encourage our own thoughts and senses to communicate with one another, and carry on this dialogue internally, within ourselves.

The first step is to permit ourselves to pause, to stop treading the spiral path of negativity, to recognize those patterns as fossils, long-vacated empty shells. We will discover, if and when we are able to do this, that energy for great creativity is released.

The next step is to engage in deep contemplation. But this doesn't necessarily mean cutting our ties, and retiring into a cave to practice. In contemplation, in deeply relaxed exploration, we draw closer and closer to the nature of mind—mind in life, in our experience, here and now.

Knowing mind can learn to contemplate itself; mind can look in its own mirror. Mind can come face to face with existing patterns and open potentials, and embrace them all. Everything that appears in that mirror is vitally important knowledge—even our flaws, even our misunderstandings.

Practice may be needed in order to stabilize this seeing. Many of us have caught glimpses of this play of mind for a few moments, but seeing will need support to carry on longer than that. It is worth patiently cultivating, for even a few minutes of this kind of contemplation can make a powerful impact on understanding.

Fortunately, there is no way to do this wrong. Reactions to seeing are part of seeing, too. Even turning away from seeing might be part of seeing, when seen in the right light. Don't give up on this project; let knowing tutor itself, until we can embrace all experience, until even our negativity opens up, revealing its hidden power and beauty. Then there is no need for walking away or walking toward, and no need to fear our own thoughts.

All our experience could be put to use, recovered and reconciled, composted and transformed. Our refining process for neurotic patterns creates energy that can power contemplation, wisdom, and compassionate action.

Even problems we feel are active right now, conditioning what is happening to us in this moment, can become integral parts of our learning if a commitment to open dialogue is patiently upheld. But this friendship with ourselves must brook no discrimination; nothing at arms'-length, no second-class-citizens in our hearts.

Our negative thoughts and feelings might be shy at first, unused to kindness. Give them a chance; it's possible they could help us. Without clouds, what understanding would we have of the sun?

Now 'cloud' becomes sunshine's witness, an emissary of joy.

In this way, encouraging ourselves and others, our outlook can fundamentally change. This is a transformation worked at a level beneath that of our daily emotional ups and downs. It gives us a cushion of patience and grace, a strong support for our compassion, and a steady supply of joy.

Perhaps it would not even be necessary to worship at temples, to idealize distant dreams of beauty and hope, if we could recognize that our own joy, our own awareness, and our own compassion are themselves sacred.

In the past, we have been so sure of ourselves—so sadly sure of our limitations.

We tend to say, "Human beings are imperfect." But we could just as easily say, "We human beings are pretty good. We're better than good—in fact, we can be great!" Accepting ourselves, respecting others, perhaps we could help the world harmonize, and practice a deeper kind of philanthropy.

If we understand how to embody knowledge, that is true service, true teaching, true leadership.

We can begin by protecting and supporting our willingness to be open to embodying knowledge. This is the foundation of all future effort. It is our seat, and in certain respects it is ordinary, as ordinary as everyday kindness. But secretly it is a throne, the indestructible throne of the awareness-holders, in whom path and goal are one.

Willingness to be present, willingness to listen, takes courage. But we can do it. We can open the lines of communication within ourselves, reversing the ordinary flow of our attention. Instead of looking for 'things going on' inside ourselves—more objects of thought to capture—we can trace the line backwards, gently following the 'from' of the 'to' into greater and greater calmness and stillness.

This change in direction doesn't just nourish us; it affects how we communicate with others, and adjusts the way we perceive all signaling. All the operations of our senses, all the ever-shifting manifestations of mind, have treasures to share.

Even Western wondering may contain many positive things, for it loves opening possibilities for human beings, and it loves creating new paths.

This kind of curiosity does not always appear in sentient beings, and even among human beings, many cultures do not reward inquisitive, speculative dreaming and desiring. When Western knowledge opens up, transcending the biases and conditions of its development, its questioning can become very precious. We must not reject it because it is 'limited', or 'technical', or '*to*-oriented'. The seeds of entirely new forms of knowledge might be waiting to arise from the transformation of the Western mind.

Even our 'how', limited as it may be, has important gifts to give.

For 'how' is dynamic and responsive. 'How' wants to be in touch, and it wants to make things happen. What if it were to use a wider compass? *How* might that work?

How do we cognize? How did this manifest? How does questioning question the questioner? Memory, that collection of marks and meanings, could be implemented here, helping us recognize our own transformations. After all, as we shift according to the rhythms of time, it is memory that builds and re-builds the baseline, allowing us to see that something has changed.

Above all, we must not treat the operations of our own minds as the enemies of our progress. These operations may be magical.

'How' treats the signals shining from space as direct communications, appeals to the self. The self-interest, the self-orientation of 'how' has struck us as a great liability, and yet perhaps even our self-interest can become an open way of conducting, when our fears and cravings are neutralized, when we recognize the mutual shining of knower and known.

Activities we have written off as part of our regime could be important friends and allies of knowledge. Consider what our labels enable us to do! Consider the tones they have taught us, the subtle differences between morning and evening light that they have helped articulate.

Instead of lining up more questions, obediently following each label's prescribed path, we could open up the label's abilities, inspiring entirely new ways for meaning to operate in our lives. Our labels could be like a painter's colors; these are means by means of which great works of art can take shape.

The operations organized by our Rule, our searching, looking, thinking, seeing, and knowing, have actually produced fruits; if we change the way we regard these pros and cons, these ratios of qualities, there is nowhere knowledge does not reside.

In our present set-up, because we are still obedient to the Rule of negation, our knowing is not omniscient. Time seems to put a veil over our seeing; the future is an unknown, and the past a little hazy. Even the present is open to question.

We have no firm conclusions, true; some might criticize us for that. Until we are entirely free, we may have a few limitations.

But there are benefits even to limits. Because we have so much to learn about time, about the operations of mind—about ourselves—we cannot just seal up any of our insights, put a stamp upon our own beliefs, ideas, and emotions. We can no longer really endorse our own dogmatism and paranoia. Even what we call 'truth' floats in time and the web of meanings; but we can let it shimmer, and learn from its movements.

Before we throw away these limitations—our practices and processes, goals and dreams, objects and subjects—let's look again; we may have missed something wonderful. The path may be conditioned by 'from' and 'to', by 'me' and 'you', but it is valuable. Without it, there is no shape, no structure, no ethics, no view, and no goal.

Can we envision uses for the self, for the 'I'?

Could I become, in purest form, a means of communication, an expressive voice, a poetic way to share love of knowledge, and knowledge of love?

Being has a close connection to great knowledge. This great knowledge has no bias; it doesn't belong to a regime. It owes nothing to the Rule, or the rules. Not even to concepts, not even to thoughts, not even to the most preliminary awareness of sound or image. It has its own freedom, its own realm: a realm without borders. This is the birthright of all sentient beings; and the greatest work we can do is to help these beings find the way home.

Home, to knowing being's imperishable kingdom, shining at the heart of time.

Chapter Eight:
The Great Journey

Introduction to Chapter Eight

In these essays, I have sometimes emphasized that we cannot rely solely on concepts and the conceptual mind. Still, we are living in this world, and our world is structured by concepts and projections. This is a reality that we cannot, in fact, deny.

We can see an acknowledgement of this truth in Buddhist teachings, which address our situation in the world as we find it. For instance, the Buddha spoke of the emptiness of all phenomena, yet he also strongly emphasized the importance of non-violence toward self and others.

As Dharma practitioners, we act to promote peace and eliminate harm: toward ourselves, toward others, and toward the natural world. This is conduct that partakes of the distinctions of the relative world, but it also strives to heal the damage caused by such distinctions. It is the best path of conduct available to us in ordinary terms.

Esoteric Mantrayana texts often emphasize that the highest teachings should be kept secret. This is not because of their difficulty, or out of any sense of shame. Instead, it is because students who lack the right preparation are likely to interpret the teachings according to the prescriptions imposed by language, and then the risk of misunderstanding is great.

For instance, when they hear that reality is without limits, they may decide that this means that karma no longer applies to them. Having heard that reality is an illusion, they may maintain that they can do whatever they wish.

Practitioners in Tibet sometimes made exactly this mistake, even some who were quite learned. They thought that they were free of all conditions, when in fact their minds were still operating at the relative level. That is why great masters were extremely cautious in deciding whom to teach and under what circumstances.

Mindful of this danger, we can choose instead to follow a balanced way. There is no mystery in this. Be kind and pleasant to others; appreciate the world your senses reveal; develop inner calm; consider your actions, and undertake them with great care.

The Nyingma monastery of Kathog, in Eastern Tibet, was founded in the twelfth century, and its monks and lamas were well-known for the power of the practice. They spent much of each day chanting mantra, cutting through thoughts and feelings and ego structures. First they penetrated the belief in a self, and then they used their realization to penetrate the appearance of solid objects such as mountains and rocks.

Sometimes monks would go off to the surrounding mountains to practice. At the end of the day, they would fly back through the sky to the monastery.

The local herdsmen had seen this happen so often that they did not pay much attention. "The yellow birds are flying," they said, "so it must be time to gather our herds and return home for the night." They had no special understanding of the Dharma or the attainments of the Sangha, but they could see with their own eyes what was happening.

The monks at Kathog could readily penetrate ordinary appearance, turning it transparent. We have evidence of their attainments, for near the monastery there was a mountain known as Monks' Robes Mountain. It had this name because the most highly accomplished monks would achieve the rainbow body at death, vanishing from the earth and leaving nothing behind but their robes. There was a cave on this mountain where people would place a stick as a marker whenever this happened, and in this way they kept a tally of how many practitioners had achieved this stage of attainment. It is said that over several centuries, the total number reached as high as a hundred thousand.

Sometimes in Tibet, practitioners acted in ways that defied convention in order to demonstrate their achievements. Because they could exercise special powers, people often accepted their claims. Yet the real proof of attainment is compassion, and real power comes from wisdom.

The masters who have reached the highest understanding most often act as ordinary people, for that is the way they can best benefit sentient beings. Jesus is known as the shepherd watching over his flock, and the followers of the Bodhisattva path act in the same way. They live with others, act with others, and provide for the needs of everyone they encounter.

Guru Padmasambhava said, "My view is higher than space, but my actions are taken with the great care, like finely ground flour." He was a master of right and wrong, and his conduct was impeccable. I believe that his is the example we should follow.

There is no contradiction here. When you are free from all forms of ignorance, when you no longer experience bias, hatred, lust, or greed and operate without a sense of 'I' and 'me' and 'mind', you are free to act from within the view of realization. But as long as we are still connected with samsara in any way, my tradition teaches that we should observe the rules that society accepts as proper, and we follow the conduct of good Dharma practitioners.

From this perspective, for those who would like to travel in the footsteps of the Lotus Guru, prayer and practice are essential. Kindness, generosity and forebearance are fundamental. We follow this course of action not to be diplomatic or because we want people to like us, but because we recognize that we still have some investments in the regime of having, being and doing; we have not yet gone beyond mind and beyond language.

My teacher, Jamyang Khyentse Chokyi Lodro, once said to me, "Do you want to know whether you have left behind samsaric attachments and samsaric beliefs? Put your hand in the fire. Then you will know."

For the sake of your own karma and the welfare of all sentient beings, balance your actions skillfully. As much as you can, manifest love and caring. Then there will be no mistakes.

The Great Journey

Our main mission in life is to be happy and healthy in body and mind, and to share our good fortune with our friends and family. Put differently, our purpose on this earth is develop what is positive and wholesome and extend that positivity out into the world.

If you think of your life as a journey by ship, it seems clear that we cannot say in advance what weather we will encounter, what kinds of waves will rock us, or what parts of the ocean we will explore. The rhythms of time manifest in the unfolding of our lives, an open process we cannot work out in advance.

In the face of so many unknowns, how can we prepare ourselves for the journey? This is a real question, one that we can explore. For instance, how can we cultivate our sensory faculties? How will we engage the structures that language establishes?

We may imagine that it is important to set a goal for our journey in advance, to know where we are headed, so that we can decide how to get there. Yet it may be more important to focus on the journey itself.

Think of the journey as a beautiful play that takes form through its own dynamic. The sounds and sights we experience, the way we communicate with our senses, the creative imagination that opens new horizons, the vision that inspires us—these are the elements that will shape the play. They can ensure that our journey will be positive, balanced, healthy, and meaningful.

When we know how to coordinate and accommodate every aspect of experience, the expressions of time unfold countless dimensions of beauty. Your responsibility is simply to play your role well, letting the ship move smoothly through the waves. Later, you can show others how to do this also, how to feel at home with the journey's rhythms.

As we have observed, experience unfolds through ripples in time: first, I notice what is happening, then I interpret what I have noticed. This back-and-forth has its own rhythm, and our interpretations reflect what has happened in different directions; each interpretation creates new potentials. If we prepare well, we can simply follow this inner dynamic, becoming aware of what we see and hear, feel and think, and how we engage the world—through encounters with others and ourselves, and in the countless situations that arise during the day.

It is natural to try to structure events and experiences in ways that offer a sense of security or protection, or to establish fixed goals or take on specific duties. Such goals and duties too are ripples, and they, too, can be embraced and integrated.

However, if we are not well prepared, if we lack understanding and wisdom, we may not be able to open wide the perceptual frame of our experience and receive what it has to offer.

You may already be familiar with the outcome of such a restriction on awareness. We have been there before. A shadow falls across each experience, leaving dark corners where no light penetrates. The result is a journey marked by emotional pain, disappointment, and disillusionment.

Unbalanced and uncomfortable, we can find ourselves lost in dreams of conflict and failure. Our interpretations offer little that is meaningful, and we may fear at a deep level that we have been wasting our time and energy.

A journey that proceeds in this way is like a jigsaw puzzle that somehow can never be put together. Trapped in thoughts and labels, you may have the sense of going in circles, with no sense of guidance. The circles become loops, and the loops grow tighter and tighter, until knowing and knowledge simply disappear. Without knowledge, there can be no joy, no light.

If this description seems accurate in any way, you already understand something about how to break out of this cycle. When we cohesively harmonize the feelings of the body, mind, and senses, opportunities for knowledge arise spontaneously.

When we are calm, loose, and open, we do not fall into bias or accept the truth of discriminating thoughts. Space opens as we do, and we can almost imagine that we are already at home in a field of bliss. We no longer find ourselves worrying about organizing our journey or pointing in a specific direction; the journey proceeds with its own joyful momentum. Joy leads us into the field of blessing; now we know how to be and what to do. Now, being opens in greater depth, a depth we discover not by busily digging deeper, but simply by opening. Confidence flows freely, showing and shining the riches of feeling that embody the bliss of blessing.

Embodied being is an important source for the knowledge that lets us return home. Such knowledge can free us from all distractions and thoughts and labels. It can transform the mind and sense faculties, like rich nectar flowing through the body. In a kind of alchemy, it can fill each point with blessings: points of seeing, points of hearing, points of tasting and touching.

When experience comes alive in this way, we naturally manifest compassion and caring. We can share with others the knowledge of how to embody rightness, how to live in accord with right thought and right intention, right speech, right action, and right livelihood, right effort, right mindfulness, and right concentration.

This is the foundation for a powerfully integrated and synchronized way of living, at peace with the environment and at one with our community. Our journey is complete, for we hold in our hand the jewel of knowledge, and we can provide for ourselves and for others whatever is needed. All poverty of mind has vanished, for there is nowhere else to go and nothing else to attain. We recognize that we ourselves embody self-realization.

Knowledge that is active in this way teaches us that the self occupies no place or point. Blessings have no borders, and as blessings unfold, each location opens onto infinity.

We may still speak of 'I' and 'me', just as the Buddha said to his disciples, "I am going to Sarnath; give me my robe." For the purpose of symbolic communication, with others and with ourselves, we eat, we sleep, we teach. But we have graduated from such samsaric structures, and we are outside the realm marked out by the four gateways.

We are no longer 'there', for there is no 'there'.

We may seem to be speaking now of a state far beyond our present way of being, but there is no real gap. We can turn each thought, each awareness, each activity of mind toward knowledge. In fact we have a kind of mission to do so, for this is the way to go beyond the conceptual and enter the realm of bliss. We proceed step by step, but we do so skillfully. The stages through which we pass become a little translucent. We are not caught up in comparisons of higher and lower, right and wrong.

Still, we may say, "I need to meditate; I need to practice; I need to go on retreat." We may have room for improvement, and for the sake of that improvement, we may use the concepts that language provides. Although knowing knows beyond mind, beyond language, and beyond concepts, conventional understanding offers consciousness the vehicle to reach this way of being.

Relative understanding can be the ship that takes us on our journey. Without it, we may have no way to go beyond samsaric structures, no way to pass through the gate of the regime of mind.

As long as we are on the path, involved in relative reality, we will know only one truth. Provided we do not cling to that truth, this is not a problem. We are simply the viewer, seeing as we see. When the viewer is gone, appearance becomes the enlightened realm; the character of what manifests does not persist, just as the pervasive, open mind of realization does not belong to its recipients.

With no audience to see or experience, the transformation is spontaneous. There is no more path and no one who practices—the journey itself is the goal of the journey, and we already hold the fruit in our hands. Until that realization dawns, however, we need the relative path; we need to follow the way of conventional understanding.

The path of relative truth is an accommodation to our ordinary understanding, presented to us through the compassion of the Bodhisattvas. Christianity says that God created the realm of form. I think this implies an understanding that the world is intrinsically holy. In a similar sense, we can say that samsara manifests solely for the purpose of liberation.

The identity of samsara and nirvana operates in both directions. Perfect realization is not separate from 'I-ness', from thoughts and the sense faculties. The path is a manifestation of enlightenment, and so is the vehicle. The method we use to obtain the result is itself the result. The journey we are on is in one sense preparation for realization; a process I need to go through to reach a different level of being.

Yet when we reach that different level, the place I began and the place I have reached are united. With no one to see them and give them identities, they are simply exhibitions of perfection. All actions—coming and going, doing and not doing—are a performance, an artistic creation, shining with aesthetic qualities. Motion, with its 'from' and 'to' is part of the rhythm of self-illumination.

While we are in the grip of karma and klesha, such unity is beyond us. Yet this does not mean that the barriers that karma and klesha erect truly have power over us. It is because in the end karma and klesha are not real that knowledge that relies on them cannot penetrate samsara. There is no Rule for nirvana.

In the course of our journey, at first we may proceed rather slowly, but then we graduate. Once we graduate, we see clearly that the unfolding of linear time and the sense of progress on a path—aspects of reality that seemed so fundamental, so vital—are in fact only *marks*, points imposed on the rhythms of time.

The marks do not mark out anything solid. There is no bridge that leads to nirvana, no carrier, no vehicle, and no road.

Marks are conditions composed in every instant. A mark that is noticed becomes a point, but a mark that opens becomes a rhythm. Yet rhythms too can turn toward the solid. They can take their part in a causal sequence, always heading toward 'next', always participating in the structure of before and after, of beginning, middle, and end. Through such structures, we 'mark out' and establish lines, which we name as moments in time.

All this unfolds in the relative world. When we stay with the open, with process and understanding, we may touch what words cannot express. Yet at the same time, we rely on words, and so we enter a world of meanings. Experientially, we see ourselves 'in' or 'on' or 'at'. We identify marks and points; we even identify *processes*, *rhythms*, and *understanding*.

Having identified, we enter the realm of 'A' and 'B', the realm of meanings such as healthy or wealthy, happy or sad, impure or annoyed. Whether we call these statuses, conditions, points, marks, or places, they establish an order, a sphere bounded by its circumference, given shape and form by the unknown.

Within this order, concepts generate boundless causal combinations. The process makes possible reasoning, grounded in 'by' and 'from' and 'to'. We identify noticing and the noticer, action and actor, and a whole range of relationships: 'next', 'first', 'last', 'in', 'by', 'on top of'. The self takes its place, and the arrow of time marks out our age, the date, and the distances in the universe.

All this depends on marks, which make possible shape and form and allow for direction, derivation, and proportion. Marks give rise to labels, meanings, concepts, visions, and feedback. The program is automatically downloaded.

From another perspective, the mark itself could be considered a combination of points and causality, like an image on a computer that arises on the basis of electrons and numerical values. The mark means that something has formed. We say, "I made that." We look for the cause, or for the process of arising, or the originating force, or for something that lies beyond. In each case, we are looking for a 'by', for the process of a product. It is through this process that the mark manifests.

Time, with its ages, its days and years, is one example. More generally, there are ratio and size. The subject-mark points out the object-mark, mark to mark. Even cognizing is 'marked out': cognizer, cognition, recognition, compiled into a focal setting, perhaps through a combination of the sensory faculties.

We can speak of all this as the field, the producer of the waves and rhythms and ripples we identify. It looks like action comes from the center of the field, but in the field, the center is centerless. Still, form manifests and creation takes form. With labels comes completion: now we can mark out the way appearance has been formed and founded.

Form is pervasive. A hundred-billionth of a nanosecond is a thing *formed*. A point is made as *formed*. Beyond form, where the power of form loosens, waves of gravity operate, invisible; yet that, too, is *formed*. It is all in the realm of knowledge and the known.

Even the unknowable, from the perspective of knowing, is a *form* of knowing. The form itself becomes the maker.

Science and religion study such subjects, but it may be a while before they reach such depths. Asking 'how' may get us closer, but there are things the 'how' cannot penetrate, for language and concepts always come up against limits.

Still, we can ask about the meaning of the mark or the point. We can also ask about the meaning of zero. When we do, new questions arise, questions that tack in new directions, asking about the other side of zero, the circumference of zero, the point of zero, the 'from' of zero, the 'to' of zero.

We could say that now we are speaking symbolically, for purposes of communication. Yet while this may be so, it is also true that appearance—as it becomes the point—becomes mysterious. Since we have not found the language to capture the meaning, we seem to have no choice: we must dismiss the meaning of points.

Yet that may not be a limitation. When we think about it, we find that we are engaging a way of life that could be called *mystical*. This is the field of our reality, the realm of body, mind, and senses, of energy, waves, and gravity, of space and knowledge. That is why we speak of it.

I hope that through our journey together, we can catch a little glimpse of the mark.

Or perhaps we can catch the *mark* of the *glimpse*.

Looking becomes the mark, and the mark marks out a symbolic gesture. Our thoughts are like that, and mind is like that as well. Waves and gravity, energy and the invisible: all interact through the forms of marks.

I do not need to hope that we enter into that understanding, for we are already part of that. It may look foreign and distant, and the words we use for pointing may seem strange, but we are part of the journey, and the journey is a part of that. It is our homeland, our relative reality, and we act upon that basis.

We may say we don't know what's going on, and it is true that there are many things we do not know. Still, knowledge grows. Two thousand years ago, there were many things not known that we know today. As soon as tomorrow, we could have a different understanding. We may have access to new information, to new rhythms of sound or images of sight. Feelings and thoughts and memories and cognitions offer so much variation that we could never record them all, yet they may never repeat. They shine, and then they are gone.

In the same way, concepts bring us all sorts of surprises—wonderful presents of knowledge. The more we watch for them, the more we look inside, the more ready we are to arrive at openness. If you accommodate appearance, loosening up and not rejecting, not freezing it in place, then things can open—like reflections in water, or the sparkle of fine, clear crystals, or the images that scamper across the surface of a mirror.

What appears may be self-reflecting. For the marks themselves can shine, and the shining itself can become knowledge. Knowledge can become borderless openness, free from bias, a deeply interesting exhibition manifesting the beauty of art, the formless form of music, and the joy of the embodiment of love.

We cannot really say what it means to go to the edge of space or capture the edge of the edge, and the same is true of knowledge. When we limit knowledge, we limit ourselves. Now we are at a time when we can open those limits. We can operate and use knowledge in a meaningful way.

We know how to do that. We do not need instructors; we do not need the constructed. The more we open knowledge, the more it shines.

Knowledge flows into knowledge. It echoes itself; it reflects itself. Knowingness becomes *knowledge-ability*, dynamic and powerful, uplifting and transforming. There are no more obstacles, no more problems, no karma and klesha. Knowing this, we can celebrate life's journey.

Please, do not forget to celebrate.

Springtime and Fourth of July Kum Nye presentation at Ratna Ling

Meditation Hall and Conference Center at Ratna Ling, established in 2004

Fourth of July Community Celebration at Ratna Ling

Daily meals and special events at Ratna Ling